THE 100-DAY DEVOTIONAL FOR BOYS

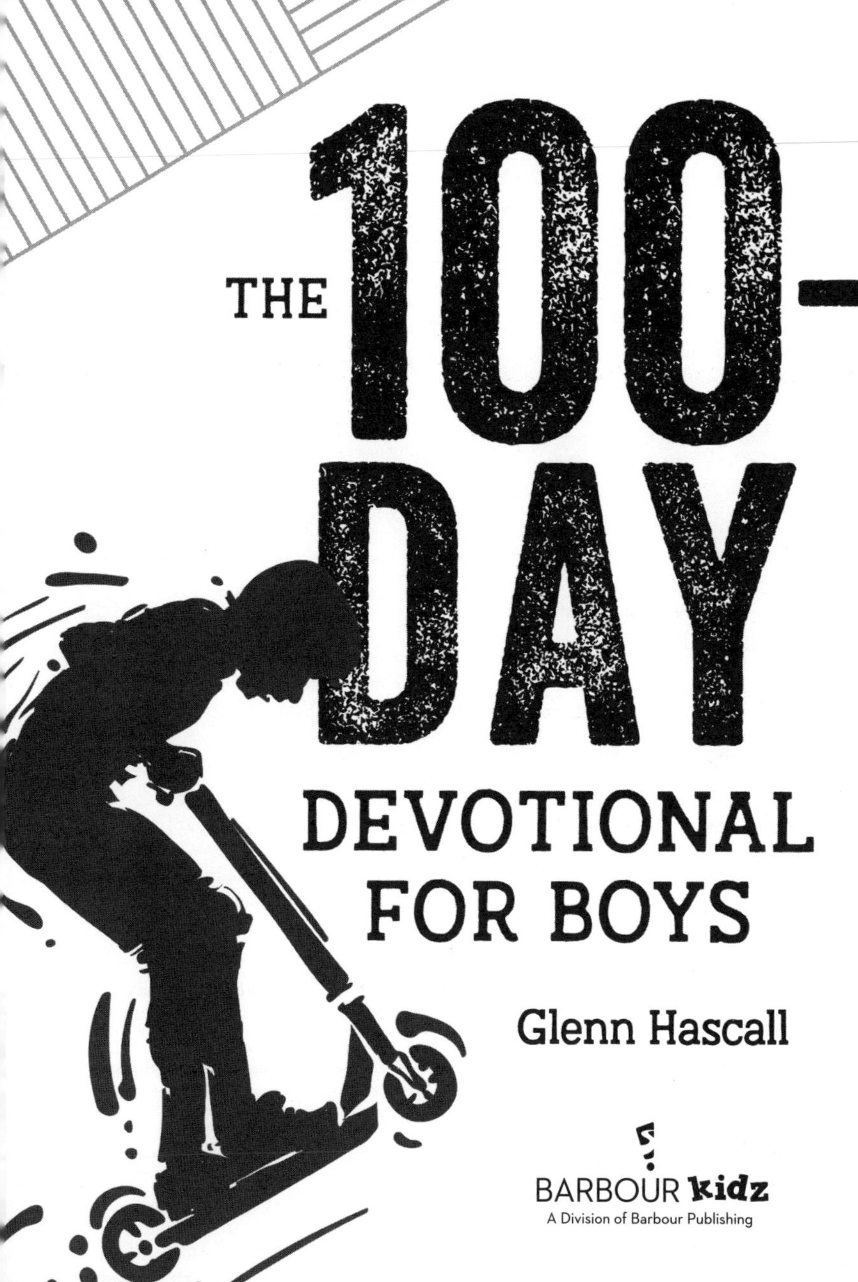

THE 100-DAY DEVOTIONAL FOR BOYS

Glenn Hascall

BARBOUR kidz
A Division of Barbour Publishing

Print ISBN 978-1-63609-570-7

Published by Barbour Publishing, Inc., 1810 Barbour Drive, Uhrichsville, Ohio 44683, www.barbourbooks.com

Our mission is to inspire the world with the life-changing message of the Bible.

Printed in China.

001569 0523 HA

HERE'S A GREAT WAY TO SPEND YOUR NEXT 100 DAYS!

On each page of this devotional, you'll discover biblical truths you can apply to every area of your life, and you'll be encouraged—each day—to grow in your faith and spend regular time in the heavenly Father's presence.

The readings touch on topics that are important to you, including:

- Boldness
- Kindness
- Serving
- Patience
- Strength
- Wisdom
- Courage
- and more!

Ready? . . . Set? . . . Turn the page to begin your 100-day adventure!

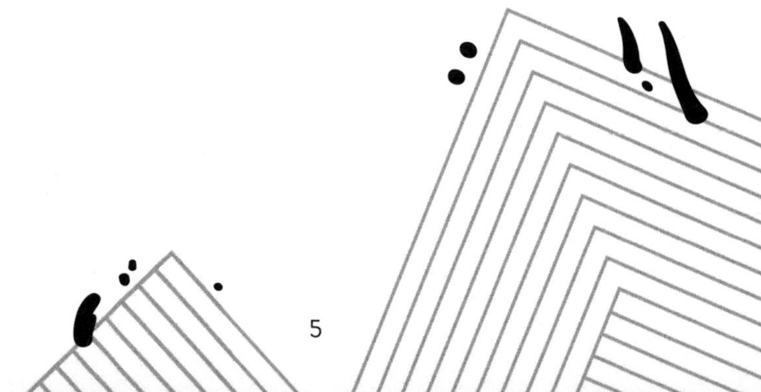

DAY 1

BEBOT'S BIG JOB

How can a young man keep his way pure? By living by Your Word.
PSALM 119:9

BeBot, a supersized robot with a big job, was a gift to the state of Florida. BeBot is like those vacuum cleaners that suck up dirt and debris from people's floors. . .but BeBot vacuums the beach instead! It separates small pieces of junk from the sand and then traps them inside its holding tank. Every day, there will be more beach trash, and BeBot will be on the job.

Sounds like a big help, right? But BeBot can't remove every speck of trash from the sand—some bits are just too small. Sure, BeBot is helpful, but it can't clean everything.

Isn't it a relief to know that God's Spirit is different? When you break God's rules and ask for His forgiveness, He makes you as clean as though you'd never sinned. *Nothing* is left behind. If you are forgiven, then God does something humans cannot—He forgets what you've done and never brings it up again. He makes things just like they were before you made the choice to sin—and He'll be back tomorrow if you need His heart- and soul-cleaning services again.

No matter how hard you try, you can't clean your heart by yourself. Only God can fix the damage done when you break His rules. Doing good things won't reverse it. Saying "I'll never do it again" won't help either. Only God can return your heart to its original, pure condition.

The best inventions are great, but they also serve as

reminders that God has always done a better job—the perfect job, in fact. The best that people can do is to try to imitate Him.

Who knew a beach vacuum named BeBot could teach us so much about God's forgiveness?

Thank You for doing such an amazing job of cleaning my heart, Lord. I don't want to stop You from making me clean. Help me remember that I can't do it on my own—I need Your help! Any time I break Your rules, I can come to You and be made clean all over again. And for that, I'm so thankful!

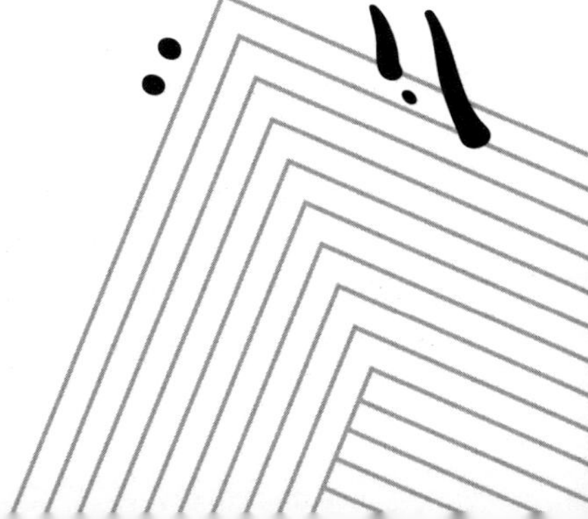

DAY 2

THE BIG PUSH

[Jesus said,] "I have done this to show you what should be done. You should do as I have done."

JOHN 13:15

Chad and his wife have five children who are all the same age because they were all born on the same day. You've probably heard of twins—two siblings born at the same time. . .but when there are five children born to the same parents at the same time, they are called *quintuplets*.

Chad has a special stroller that allows him to push all five children at once. This would be impressive enough at the mall or an amusement park, but Chad took them to a half-marathon he was running in California. For more than two hours, this dad ran with all five of his children until he crossed the finish line! Whether the four-year-olds clapped at the finish or looked around in confusion, one thing is certain: this stroller ride was one they'll never forget! Chad hopes that at least a few of his children will decide to run alongside him when they get older. His goal is to set a positive example that his quintuplets can follow.

God has done the same thing for you by setting an example. He never asks you to do things He doesn't do. That way, He makes sure you have His perfect example to follow. You get to make that choice, of course, but God will always be there, doing good things right along with you to show you that His way really is the best. God doesn't just say, "Do what I say!" Nope. He wants you to be kind, loving, and willing to forgive because He's kind, loving, and willing to forgive too.

You get to live an incredible adventure because God gives you something to do every single day—and then He gives you the choice of whether you'll do it.

You have some big decisions to make, so be sure you're following the right example!

My choices are important, Father. If I pay attention, I will see what You do, and then it will be clear that I should do the same. Help me stay focused on You so that I can recognize Your example, Lord. Help me do everything You're asking me to do.

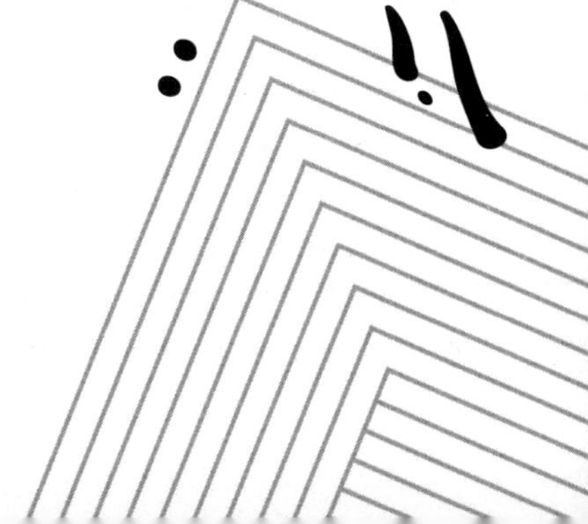

DAY 3

THE WAFFLE DAY PROBLEM

At one time you lived in darkness. Now you are living in the light that comes from the Lord. Live as children who have the light of the Lord in them. This light gives us truth. It makes us right with God and makes us good.

Ephesians 5:8–9

People make mistakes all the time. Someone who's making a sign might misspell a word. Someone putting a toy together might misunderstand part of the instructions, causing the toy to not work properly.

In Sweden, someone once made a mistake while naming a holiday. The Swedish word that person chose for the holiday was *Våffeldagen*, a religious word. However, when people heard that particular word spoken, they thought people were saying "waffles." As a result, there is now an annual Waffle Day that many countries celebrate. Some people who know what that word means celebrate the religious part of the special day. . .but others celebrate by just eating waffles.

Everybody—including you—makes mistakes. We miss test questions, fail games, or say the wrong things. Mistakes often happen because of things you don't know or can't remember.

Sin, however, is when you break God's rules. That sounds like a mistake, doesn't it? Not exactly. Sin is *more* than just a mistake. Sin can't be blamed on what you don't know, because God's rules are in the Bible—so you *can* know. The Bible is God's rulebook that teaches you everything He wants you to do. All you have to do is read it and then do what it says!

You should apologize for many mistakes, but sin *always* requires forgiveness. Thankfully, that's just what God offers!

Accept His offer today. Be a boy who is loved—and forgiven—by God.

It's easier to admit a mistake than to admit that I broke Your rules, God. Mistakes mean that I am learning. But when I break Your rules, it means I made a choice to disobey—and that's more than just a mistake. Help me treat our relationship better than that, God. When I fail, I want to be quick to let You know that I blew it.

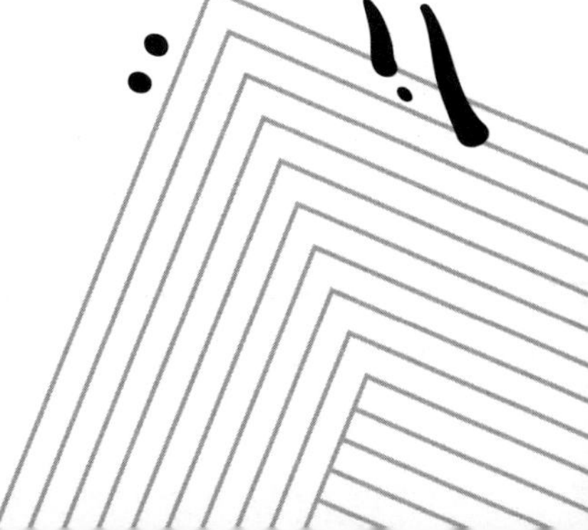

DAY 4

THE TREASURE DETECTOR

[Jesus said,] "Do not gather together for yourself riches of this earth. They will be eaten by bugs and become rusted. Men can break in and steal them. Gather together riches in heaven where they will not be eaten by bugs or become rusted. Men cannot break in and steal them. For wherever your riches are, your heart will be there also."

MATTHEW 6:19–21

On a beach on the east coast of the United States, Craig walked along with his trusty metal detector. This machine could help him find buried treasure by detecting coins, rings, or even just bottle caps under the sand. Suddenly, his detector beeped and blipped—something worth discovering was buried there. After digging four feet into the dry sand, Craig found a metal ball covered in mud. Little did he know, this was a cannonball from the 1700s! The historic treasure was then brought to the surface and photographed.

Craig had spent lots of time and money to find treasure. Why? Because that's what treasure-hunters do.

You can be a treasure-hunter too! Start with the Bible. The Bible's words are like a treasure map, helping you know where to go, what to do, and what to seek out. This treasure is worth more than all the money in the world. No one can steal or sell it. And amazingly, you can carry this treasure with you everywhere you go and even tell people where to find it for themselves. It's a treasure available to everyone!

Use your heart, mind, soul, and strength to search for God's treasure that lasts forever. There's more than enough of His love to go around, so every single person on earth can become one of His treasure-hunters too!

Your Word is my greatest treasure, Lord. Detecting You has been my greatest discovery. Help me remember this when it seems like stuff I can buy is more important than You. Give me a mind that thinks about You, a heart that wants to please You, a spirit that learns from You, and a soul that longs to be with You. My treasure has been detected. Let it make a lifelong difference in me.

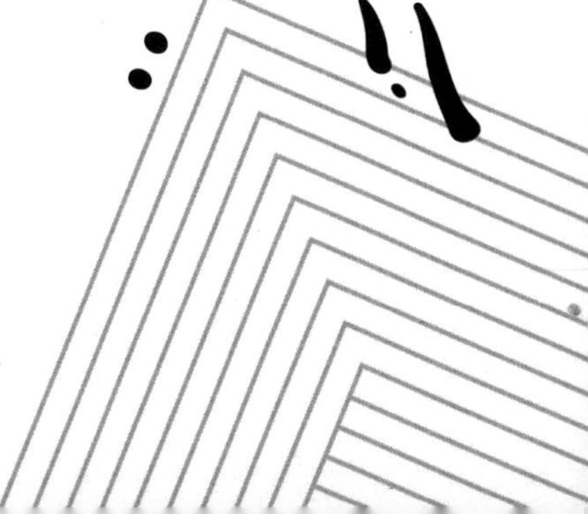

DAY 5

BUNNY'S DAY OUT

"My son was. . .lost and now he is found. Let us eat and have a good time."
LUKE 15:24

Have you ever heard a story that just made you feel good? Here's one of those feel-good stories.

At an airport in Virginia, a little girl discovered that her stuffed bunny was missing. You probably know what it's like to lose a favorite toy, right? If you can't find it for a certain length of time, nothing feels quite right for a while. Sometimes, you may even feel so sad that tears start gathering in the corners of your eyes. This little girl needed to feel better—but until the bunny was found, that wasn't going to happen.

Some workers at the airport eventually found the bunny. Knowing that it must've belonged to a child, they started moving the bunny around to different places in the airport, taking pictures and posting them on social media. (Sounds like the bunny was having a great time!) Soon, this extra effort brought the beloved bunny back into the arms of its rightful owner.

In the Bible, Jesus tells a feel-good story like this.

A dad thought he'd lost his son for good. The son took his inheritance—family money passed on to future generations—and moved far away. The father didn't hear from his son. He didn't know where he was staying and wasn't sure he'd ever return home.

But eventually, the son grew tired of his lifestyle and

remembered how good he'd had it at home. He wondered how his dad would treat him when he returned. Would he be mad? Would he even want his son to come home?

The son decided to travel back home anyway. When the father saw his son, what do you think he did? He ran to meet him, prepared a nice meal, and welcomed his son back into the family with a joyful celebration!

Just like the little girl wanted her lost bunny. . .and just like the father missed his son. . .God wants you home with Him. If you're lost—or even if you try to run away from Him—God knows where you are, and He'll wait for you to return to Him. And once you do, He will make you feel welcomed and loved.

I don't want to run and hide, Father. I don't want to make You wait to hear from me. Help me return to You when my choices take me in the wrong direction. Thanks for always welcoming me home!

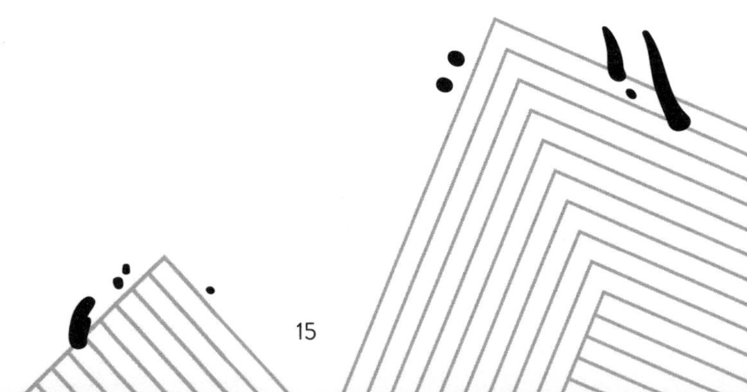

DAY 6

THE SPIRITUAL EXOSKELETON

[God] gives strength to the weak. And He gives power to him who has little strength. Even very young men get tired and become weak and strong young men trip and fall. But they who wait upon the Lord will get new strength. They will rise up with wings like eagles. They will run and not get tired. They will walk and not become weak.

Isaiah 40:29–31

Simon likes to walk, but it's not easy for him. You see, Simon is paralyzed. This means that part of Simon's body can't do what most bodies can, so he isn't able to walk on his own. Doctors gave him what they call an *exoskeleton*—a device Simon can wear on the outside of his body that helps him move his legs. When he wears the exoskeleton, Simon can walk! Sounds like something from a sci-fi movie, doesn't it? But Simon has been using the exoskeleton for a few years now. He's even completed a marathon and climbed all 1,444 steps of a skyscraper in England—a new record for the greatest number of steps climbed by someone with an exoskeleton. Pretty incredible for a man who can't walk on his own!

Just as Simon needs help to walk, you also need help to do everything God asks you to do. In fact, some things are impossible without Him. So what should you do? Let God equip you. Like the exoskeleton helps Simon, God helps you take seemingly impossible steps in this great life adventure. Without Him, you can never find your place in God's amazing race.

Remember: You are weak; God is strong. And He will strengthen and equip you to do more than you ever dreamed. Whatever good you accomplish, it won't be because you tried harder than everyone else. Nope, it'll be because God offered to help and you responded, "Yes, God, I accept!"

You have things for me to do, God. I need Your help, so please make me wise enough to ask for it. When You offer to help me, I will say yes. I want to do big things. And I can—I will!—with Your help.

DAY 7

YOU'RE MORE THAN A MASCOT

All things are pure to the man with a pure heart. But to sinful people nothing is pure. Both their minds and their hearts are bad. They say they know God, but by the way they act, they show that they do not. They are sinful people. They will not obey and are of no use for any good work.

Titus 1:15–16

If you go to watch your favorite sports team, you'll probably see a mascot—an animal, person, or object that represents the team. If a team is called the Bears, their mascot is a bear. If a team is called the Eagles, then the mascot is an eagle. Typically, a person dressed up in a mascot costume will provide entertainment and cheer alongside fans at a sporting event. Mascots are super good at playing pretend.

While it had nothing to do with mascots, 252 people in Ireland decided in 2022 to put on golden lion costumes—complete with manes and tails—and gathered together to try for a world record. There has never been a time when so many people have gathered in one place dressed as lions. It had to be fun, being in a group with so many people pretending!

Every day of the year, people pretend to be something they're not. But many of them aren't pretending for fun or to set a world record—some of them are pretending for very selfish reasons. The Bible includes true stories about people who *said* they knew and followed God—but it wasn't true. They were just actors. They talked about how great God was, but then they broke His rules whenever they could. These people played pretend for all the wrong reasons.

God wants your words to match how you live. If they don't, you're not being truthful.

When you accept God into your heart, you become His child. You're not just a mascot on the sidelines playing pretend. So get out on the field! Follow God's lead and live for Him every single day.

I don't want to pretend to know You, Lord. I want to REALLY know You, follow You, and live however You want me to. Help my actions follow my words. Thank You.

DAY 8

LESSONS FROM A DONKEY WRANGLING

Let us keep looking to Jesus. Our faith comes from Him and He is the One Who makes it perfect.

HEBREWS 12:2

Brian is a police officer who gets called to all kinds of emergency situations. One day, he was dispatched to capture a donkey named Kevin who had escaped from his enclosure in California.

When Brian arrived on the scene, it seemed Kevin didn't want to be captured. His ears were pointed backward, and he looked like he was ready to run. Kevin stared at Brian; Brian stared back at the donkey. Slowly, the donkey's ears relaxed, and he surrendered. He then let Brian lead him back to his enclosure.

Perhaps Kevin was simply more interested in exploring the other side of the fence than he was in running away from police. Some of the people who saw the donkey wrangling said they thought Brian's mustache was what calmed the donkey down and made him stop running. Kevin seemed to respect a man with a mustache.

Although this story is funny, we can all act a lot like Kevin from time to time. Sometimes, we're tempted to run away from God's plan and refuse to surrender. But when God shows up, we can either calm down or run. When we keep our eyes on Him, that's when we see that His love invites us to stop running and come back to His safety, where we are meant to be.

Jesus wants to be your primary focus. Running away and being stubborn like Kevin doesn't help you focus on Him—it only adds to the distractions. Keep paying attention to Jesus and you just might find that what He offers you is so much better than anything you might discover when you're on the run.

Sometimes, I think I know more than You do, Father. But I don't—and I never will. The reason I think this way is usually because I'm not paying attention to what You're teaching. It's very easy for me to get distracted. Remind me to keep my focus on You—even though I can't physically see You. I know I'll always be safe with You!

DAY 9

TRUTH IN THE GARDEN

Do not worry. Learn to pray about everything.
Give thanks to God as you ask Him for what you need.
PHILIPPIANS 4:6

Sometimes, things aren't what they seem. Residents of Oldham, England, were surprised to see a tiger lying peacefully in the public garden. If they thought the animal would leave on its own, they were wrong. The animal seemed content to stay in the shade of the quiet garden.

The longer the people watched, the more they worried. After all, a tiger could hurt someone! No one could feel safe knowing a tiger was running wild in the streets. Something needed to be done.

The concerned citizens called the police, who took the call very seriously. Many officers responded. Step by step, the officers cautiously headed into the garden. As they approached, the tiger made no sounds and didn't move a muscle. The officers were confused—shouldn't this tiger react in some way to their presence in the garden? Imagine the surprise (and relief!) when the officers discovered the tiger was only a giant stuffed animal someone had placed in the garden!

Often, we worry when we don't fully understand a situation. God, however, wants you to know that all the things you spend time worrying about are just like that stuffed tiger. When you have Him on your side, what room is there for worry? Even when things look big and scary, remember that God is always bigger and more powerful. When God is with you, He always wins.

What a relief!

When you're worried, take a time-out. Ask yourself: Who's bigger than God? When you have the right answer—*nothing*—all your worries will melt away. Pray and thank God for always taking care of everything—even big tigers in quiet gardens!

Trusting You is so much better than worrying about things I can't control, God. Help me take time to listen for Your voice when I pray so that I can discover how much You've always cared. Help me understand that You're here to help me when I'm sad, lonely, or confused. Your love is bigger than anything I'm afraid of. Thank You!

DAY 10

DREAMING BIG

Think of other people as more important than yourself.
PHILIPPIANS 2:3

Most people will graduate from high school before they are 20 years old. Some might get a diploma a little later because they need to complete more classes after their senior year. But few (if any) have waited as long for their diploma as Merrill.

When Merrill was a senior in high school back in the 1930s, his mom had to move away, and he never completed high school. Merrill always wanted to go back and earn his diploma, but things always seemed to get in the way of his goal. So for more than 80 years, he kept hoping and wishing. Then the unexpected happened. When Merrill turned 101 years old, his school remembered Merrill from a visit he'd made there a few years before. During his visit, he'd mentioned how sad he was that he'd never gotten his diploma. So the school did something amazing—they surprised Merrill with an honorary diploma. . .and even had a graduation ceremony for him! As Merrill walked the stage in a cap and gown, everything seemed right in his world.

People's big hopes and dreams don't always work out the way they want, no matter how much they've planned. Obstacle after obstacle seems to block the way, making those dreams seem impossible. But what if God wanted you to encourage the dreams of others? What if you could find ways to help them reach their goals? What if people just needed to know you believed in them—that you had their back?

God has put so many people in your life to help you achieve your hopes and dreams and to cheer you on along the way. Adults who give good advice, friends who encourage you, teachers who help you learn new things. . .the list goes on. When people help you reach the goals you set for yourself, it gives you the courage and motivation to keep pressing forward—and helps you pass that enthusiasm to others!

You want Christians to encourage each other, Lord, but I'm not always good at it. Remind me that when I'm encouraged, it helps me keep doing the hard work that will help me reach my goals. If that's true for me, then I'm pretty sure it's true for everyone I know.

DAY 11

BATTERED BUT BLESSED

My Christian brothers, what good does it do if you say you have faith but do not do things that prove you have faith? Can that kind of faith save you from the punishment of sin? What if a Christian does not have clothes or food? And one of you says to him, "Goodbye, keep yourself warm and eat well." But if you do not give him what he needs, how does that help him? A faith that does not do things is a dead faith.

James 2:14–17

Riley didn't realize the danger he faced. As he drove his bright red truck into a storm after a job interview, he had no idea that the storm was a tornado! The tornado shoved his ten-year-old truck around and tipped it on its side. But then a miracle happened! The wind pushed his truck back up on four wheels, and Riley was able to drive the battered truck out of the tornado's path.

Although Riley's truck was totaled in the storm, the vehicle saved him from complete disaster. He felt that God was giving him a second chance. To Riley's surprise, a local auto dealership gave him a new truck, and people in his community helped pay for his medical bills. After the accident, Riley discovered he had more friends than he thought.

The way friends and neighbors responded to Riley is a perfect example of how God wants Christians to respond to other people's struggles. God wants His children to do more than just say, "That's too bad" or "I'll pray for you"—He wants us to take action and help!

Disasters will happen—and God uses other people to help. When you pitch in and help someone in need, you're helping others notice the light of God. When you refuse to help, you're not helping others see Him and His goodness.

Remember how Riley thought God was giving him a second chance? Maybe he was encouraged to think this way when he saw how much people cared.

Help in action makes a very big difference!

You help people like me, Father, and then You ask me to help others. Thank You for being my example and believing in me enough that You ask me to follow You. Help me make the right choice and say yes.

DAY 12

HE SPOKE TRUTH

I have looked with care into these things from the beginning. I have decided it would be good to write them to you one after the other the way they happened. Then you can be sure you know the truth about the things you have been taught.

LUKE 1:3-4

Have you ever heard of a "Christian worldview"? It's what Christians believe that helps them understand the world they live in. This is important to remember.

Not long ago, a large group of people were asked whether they believe God is real, if the Bible is filled with God's words, and whether they do what the Bible says to do. Only 6 out of every 100 people who filled out the survey said yes to all those things. That's not very many, is it?

If you're holding this book, it's probably because someone cares about you and wants you to learn more about God and His Word. When you're influenced by a Christian worldview, it can change what you believe, the words you speak, and the choices you make.

God doesn't lie. There's nothing in the Bible that isn't true. He isn't playing a game of "True or False." The Bible says that it's God's kindness that makes people want to know Him. Telling the truth is loving and kind, but how kind would it be to lie—and then keep lying—to people? Jesus said in Luke 1:4 that you can confidently know the truth. Truth comes from God—so if it's from Him, you can be sure it's right!

God wants you to trust Him. So why would He betray your trust by lying to you? You might not always understand God, but you will never catch Him in a lie. God has always been completely honest, and He's not interested in changing the Bible simply because some people don't like what it says.

Thank Him today for always telling the truth!

It only makes sense that You would tell me the truth, God. You will never play a prank on me or leave me feeling confused about what to believe. Your Word is full of Your directions for the very best way to live. You speak truth—help me live like I believe it.

DAY 13

A KINDNESS SURPRISE

God has chosen you. You are holy and loved by Him. Because of this, your new life should be full of loving-pity. You should be kind to others and have no pride. Be gentle and be willing to wait for others.

Colossians 3:12

An act of kindness was captured on video, and this video went viral. It doesn't show the people's faces very well, but you can clearly hear their conversation. A customer asked for some water, and the owner made sure he got a drink. The customer then asked if he could get a sandwich—but suddenly realized he didn't have the money to pay for it. He would have to go home and get the money and come back later. The owner didn't hesitate—he quickly made a sandwich for the man.

But then came the surprise: the customer had actually planned it all out! He had gone into the shop to see what would happen if he asked for a drink and some food with no money. If the owner showed him kindness even when he didn't have to, the customer planned to award him 500 dollars.

Kindness is shown in the things we say and the things we do. When you show people kindness, they might never say thank you. . .or they could surprise you with gratitude. When you read Colossians 3:12, you'll learn these important things: you are holy, you are loved by God, your life should be full of loving-kindness, you should be humble (not full of pride), you should be gentle, and you should be willing to wait for others. It *doesn't* say that you should expect to get 500 dollars in return.

When you're kind, it's really neat to see others following your example. Kindness is contagious—it seems to inspire other people to show kindness as well. Kindness is one of the ways God can move love from His heart to your heart—and then to the hearts of others.

Being kind shows others that God's love is real and worth trusting.

Sometimes, I only want to do things that make life better for me, Lord. If I choose to be kind, then I need to think about things that will make life better for others. Your kindness helped me, and I want my kindness to help others. I am thankful for You, Lord.

DAY 14

A BETTER COLLECTION

"Do not gather together for yourself riches of this earth. They will be eaten by bugs and become rusted. Men can break in and steal them. Gather together riches in heaven where they will not be eaten by bugs or become rusted. Men cannot break in and steal them. For wherever your riches are, your heart will be there also."

Matthew 6:19–21

Charlotte has a very unusual collection. It's not a collection of toys or music boxes, cars or elephant statues—it's not even something she wears or puts on a shelf for other people to see. For the last ten years, Charlotte has been working to remove little metal balls from the tips of writing pens. She places them in a box and then puts the box in a drawer. They hold meaning for Charlotte. . .but they don't have much meaning for anyone else. No one asks to see her collection because most people have no idea that she is a collector.

Do you collect anything? Cards? Baseballs? Video games? Whatever's in your collection, it's probably as important to you as those little metal balls are to Charlotte.

While there's nothing wrong with collecting things, God wants you to know there's something much more important than any collection. You see, when it's time to go to heaven, you can't take anything—not even your collections—with you. Someone else will get everything you leave behind. But the good, God-honoring choices you make will last forever. They are a collection that has purpose and meaning.

God's good collection will last forever and will always be yours. It won't rust, rot, or fall apart. When you make good choices, it shows that you understand that earthly treasure and heavenly treasures are very different. Choose to collect heavenly, lasting treasures today!

The things I think are incredible right now won't last forever, Father. Help me remember that even though I can enjoy things, I can't live without You. Help me walk closely with You every single day. Keep me walking patiently toward a better collection—a lasting treasure in heaven!

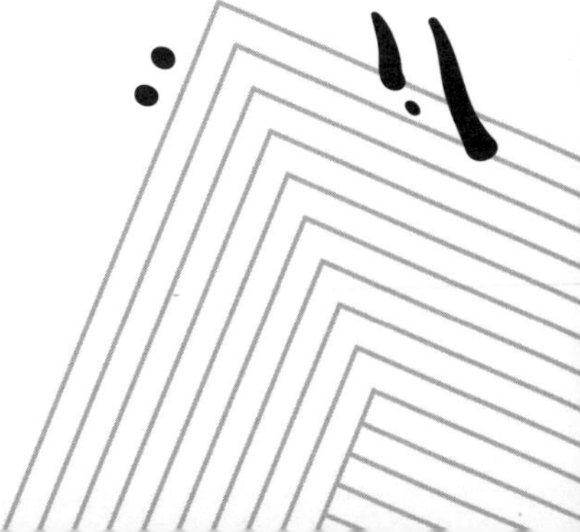

DAY 15

NO FEAR IN KNOWING

"Do not fear, for I am with you. Do not be afraid, for I am your God. I will give you strength, and for sure I will help you. Yes, I will hold you up with My right hand that is right and good."

Isaiah 41:10

Alex lives in Australia and loves to take relaxing walks on the beach. But one day, his walk wasn't so relaxing. He stumbled across a beast so unusual he wasn't quite sure what he was looking at. It didn't look human, but it wasn't like any animal he'd ever seen. He soon began to have frantic thoughts. *Did an alien die and wash up on the beach?*

The beast, Alex said, had four hands and a reptile head and tail. Once word about the strange creature got out, Professor Stephanie from a nearby Australian university set things straight. What Alex had found was a swollen, soaking wet brushtail possum. The professor's findings relieved a lot of stress for Alex—and for anyone else who had heard the story.

Does anything stress you out? Sometimes, you see, hear, and believe things you're not sure are true. Your brain tells you they are, however, so you worry and get completely stressed out because what you think is real may not be the truth. Your mind won't stop racing until you make a choice about it—and often, that choice is rushed and unwise.

It's important—to you, your family, your friends, and God—that you know the truth. Prayer, a trusted adult, and the Bible can help you with this. God, after all, never wants you to believe a lie.

Like Alex, you might believe—or even fear—something that just isn't true. Trust God to help you learn truth so that you can easily tell when a lie washes up. Ask Him for wisdom today. . .and He'll give it!

I need to know the truth, God. I don't want to experience fear and anxiety because of lies. I know You'll never lie to me, so I want more of You in my life. With You by my side, I'll believe what You say, do what You ask, and go where You send me.

DAY 16

LAWS TO OBEY

The Law of the Lord is perfect, giving new strength to the soul. The Law He has made known is sure, making the child-like wise.
Psalm 19:7

Everywhere people live has laws—rules you need to obey. Some laws may seem strange.

North Carolina has a few of those unusual laws. For instance, if you're tempted to take kitchen grease that isn't yours, don't—it's a crime! If you're caught, a punishment is given. . .based on how much kitchen grease you stole. It's also a crime in the state to borrow a neighbor's dog, horse, or mule without permission. And if you're looking for fun things to do in North Carolina, make sure you don't drive on the sidewalks—that will get you into trouble too!

God also has laws. He wants you to pay attention to them, learn what they are, and follow them. He wants you to trust that He's wise enough to be fair, strong enough to judge law-breakers, and loving enough to forgive. And if you ever believe for even a minute that following God's laws isn't worth it, think again! His rules are *always* worth following—they simply make life better. If you have trouble following any of His laws, God promises to help you. Just ask.

When you break one of God's laws, you are guilty. But there's good news! God sent His Son, Jesus, to take your guilt away. He forgives. He forgets. He loves you! So when you mess up, be sure to talk to God and tell Him you're sorry!

What you believe about God's laws is important. They aren't suggestions to follow when you feel like it, and they'll never go out of date. Following God's laws will always draw you closer to Him. Choose to follow them today—and all your days to come!

Lord, You didn't give laws for me to ignore—You want me to obey them. When I follow Your laws, it shows I'm willing to choose and follow You. So even when I don't understand why You want me to do something, help me to obey because You asked. Thank You!

DAY 17

NO CLIPPED WINGS

Christian brother, you were chosen to be free. Be careful that you do not please your old selves by sinning because you are free. Live this free life by loving and helping others.

GALATIANS 5:13

When you go to a zoo, you expect to see animals, reptiles, and birds. . .but what happens if an animal escapes? Well, you expect animal experts to track them down and bring them back.

Many years ago, several flamingos were brought to a zoo in Wichita, Kansas. Zoo staff planned to clip their wings so that they would stay on the zoo property. But before they could do that, two flamingos escaped. One of them has a band around its leg that shows the number 492, and it's been spotted in several states.

After nearly 20 years, this bird was spotted again in Texas. Workers at the zoo, however, say they will not try to bring it back. The bird has been free for a very long time, so why would they disturb it by caging it up? Besides, flamingos can live to be 70 years old, so 492 could have many more years to explore the world.

Did you know that God made you to be free? He doesn't clip your wings; instead, the boundaries He sets allow you to discover something far better than the freedom to do whatever you want. You have the freedom to do what God *created* you to do.

You were made to refuse sin. Sin, after all, never really

allowed you to soar. You were made to go on an adventure with Jesus—to be more than an example of sin that others can watch. God wants you to rise above that choice.

Your wings aren't clipped, and you don't live in a cage. Go where God sends you and do what He asks. There's a lot you can do on this wonderful quest.

God helped you escape, so why would you ever return to the zoo?

Thank You for making me free, Father. Help me hold tight to this new life and enjoy the places You take me and the things You want to teach me. I'm free when I'm with You and a slave when I'm not. Help me to stay where You are.

DAY 18

BETTER THAN A FURRY OWL RODENT

"I know the plans I have for you," says the Lord, "plans for well-being and not for trouble, to give you a future and a hope."
JEREMIAH 29:11

There was a toy in the 1990s that everyone—maybe even your parents—wanted at the time. They looked like a cross between an owl and a rodent. When you touched them, they would speak gibberish.

These toys were extremely popular, and for a while, they were very hard to find. But not everyone liked them. The National Security Agency (NSA) didn't want the toy in their offices because they believed it could record their secret conversations and pass them along to spies. Soon, parents became concerned. Some got rid of the cute, fur-covered toy.

No one could prove this toy was stealing secrets, however, and some adults still have them boxed up in their attics.

Privacy might be important to you. Bedrooms usually have doors, and you probably wouldn't like to share *everything* that's on your mind. But God sees what happens when you close your bedroom door, and He knows what you're thinking. Even more, He uses what He knows to teach you and bring you closer to Him. You may have questions that never reach your lips, but He hears them. He's not a toy. . .but you should want Him. Out of all the millions of prayers offered up every day, He takes time to listen to you too.

Unlike this toy, God is always available. He answers the

minute you call, and He helps the minute you ask. You may not hear actual words, but He will tell you what you need to know through the Bible. He is the best gift you can receive. . .and the best gift you'll ever share.

You know me so well, God. I can't hide anything from You, but You love me anyway. I break Your laws, but when I admit I was wrong and You were right, You forgive me. I can't run far enough, fast enough, or long enough to leave You behind. You're with me, and I'm better because You have agreed to make me new. I don't want to make it hard for You to change me. Help me cooperate with You.

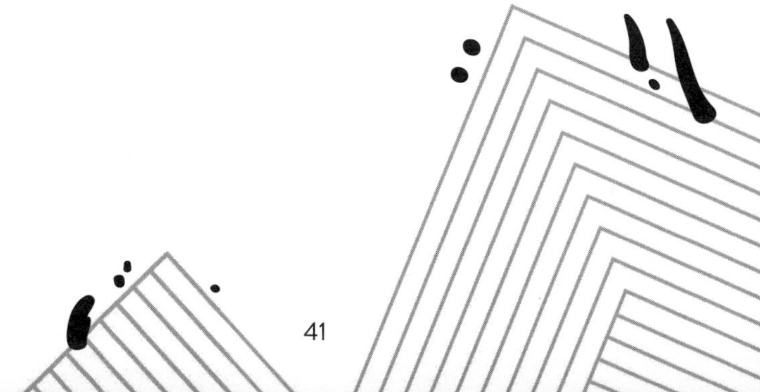

DAY 19

GOD'S PLAN IS AMAZING

"Walk in all the way the Lord your God has told you. Then you may live, it may be well with you, and you may live a long time."
DEUTERONOMY 5:33

Being a Christian might make you healthier and give you a longer life. Experts found that people who said they went to church live longer than those who don't.

The reason for this? No one knows for sure! Maybe it's because if you trust God instead of worrying, then you'll have less stress. Or maybe when you obey God, you'll be less interested in breaking His rules, and that can help protect you.

Following God doesn't guarantee a long life—experts just agree that there's a connection more often than not. This is one of the good things you might find when you follow God.

Here is a top five list of other benefits of following God.

1. *God is trustworthy:* "We can trust God that He will do what He promised" (Hebrews 10:23).
2. *God keeps His promises:* "Every good promise which the Lord had made to the people of Israel came true" (Joshua 21:45).
3. *God is kind:* "The fruit that comes from having the Holy Spirit in our lives is: love, joy, peace, not giving up, being kind, being good, having faith, being gentle, and being the boss over our own desires. The Law is not against these things" (Galatians 5:22–23).

4. *God gives you purpose:* "We are His work. He has made us to belong to Christ Jesus so we can work for Him" (Ephesians 2:10).
5. *God is with you:* "Be strong and have strength of heart! Do not be afraid or lose faith. For the Lord your God is with you anywhere you go" (Joshua 1:9).

And here are five more: *God is good* (Psalm 119:68). *God gives you strength* (2 Timothy 1:7). *God can make you wise* (James 1:5). *God's love is forever* (Romans 8:38–39). *God brings you joy* (Psalm 16:11).

With all these reasons, why would anyone want to avoid serving God?

You give amazing gifts, Lord. Help me remember them and know that You want me to live a very good life by following a very good God.

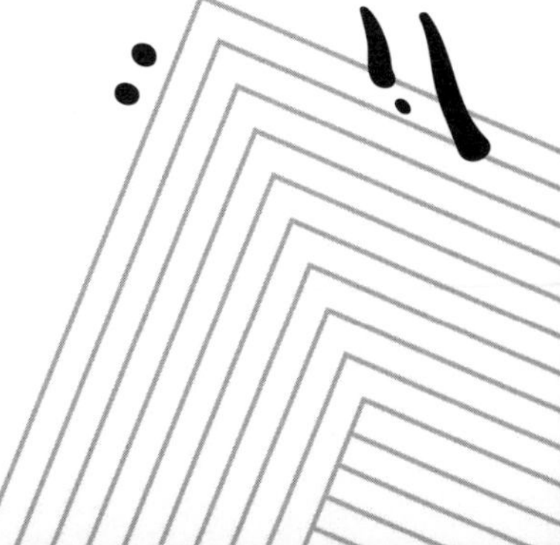

DAY 20

THE TREASURE SEEKER FINDS

"The holy nation of heaven is like a man who buys and sells. He is looking for good pearls. When he finds one good pearl worth much money, he goes and sells all that he has and buys it."

Matthew 13:45–46

George Henderson could've been playing basketball in the driveway or a video game with his friends. He could've been reading or trying out some new jokes with his friends. But George craved adventure. His dad introduced him to treasure hunting, and the things he's found has kept this ten-year-old busy for half his life. He lives in Europe, and when he went exploring one autumn day, George found an artifact that sold for more than 5,000 dollars!

This young man was hunting on land he didn't own. But before he started, he did two things: (1) he got permission, and (2) he promised that if he found anything worthwhile, he would share the sale price with the farmer who owned the land.

George lived up to the promise, so a farmer with a hidden, centuries-old artifact now has some extra cash.

Jesus gave up everything to reach you, and it's worth doing the same to get Him. Jesus said that finding Him was like finding a treasure. In fact, He's greater than any treasure on earth! Seeking Him is worth the adventure, and finding Him is an experience like no other.

George will have a great story—and some great memories—for the rest of his life. He will remember the value of what he found. A farmer also got to see the treasure, so he will always remember that it came from his land. He'll be thankful for the money he received, and it's possible he'll be friends with George for a very long time.

Seek God. Expect treasure. Let God take care of it for you. Then? Remember.

I will seek treasure that only comes from You, Father. If I keep looking, I will find what You've promised. Your treasure doesn't wear out or break. It's never worth less than it was when You gave it. Help me share it with someone today.

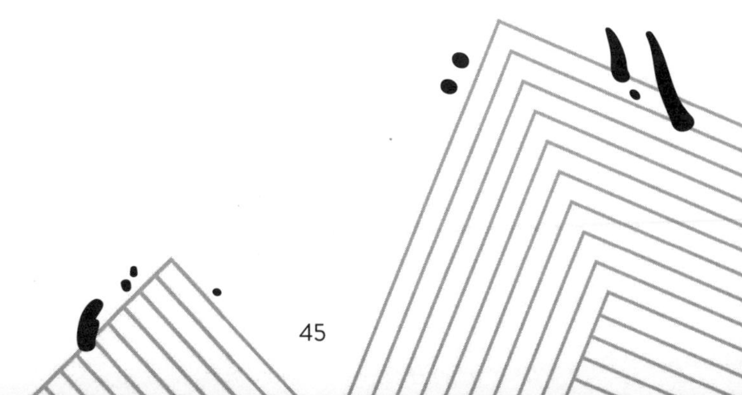

DAY 21

BE AN EXAMPLE—NO WAITING REQUIRED

Tell people that this is what they must do. Let no one show little respect for you because you are young. Show other Christians how to live by your life. They should be able to follow you in the way you talk and in what you do. Show them how to live in faith and in love and in holy living.

1 Timothy 4:11–12

Chris is a professor with lots of responsibilities, but he still remembers his tenth-grade year in high school. That's when he started work at an Indiana pharmacy. He was a *soda jerk*—someone who would make all the soda-based products customers wanted, from ice cream to hand-crafted shakes. Chris worked there for three years before he left for college.

Apparently, you can take the boy out of the soda shop, but you can't take the soda shop out of the boy. Even after becoming an adult, Chris never stopped thinking about his job in the pharmacy. So when Chris learned that the equipment he had used back in the 1980s was up for sale, he bought it. What would a grown-up professor do with old soda equipment? Chris turned his garage into a replica of the pharmacy soda shop, and he makes sodas for family and friends.

Today, you can get to know God—you don't have to wait. And when you become an adult, you don't have to leave Him behind. Some people try that and later regret it. Following

God isn't just for children; you can walk with God every day of your life, letting your life be an example for other people who may have forgotten how amazing God is.

God thought this truth was so important that He put it in the Bible. Boys like you don't have to wait to share what they know about God.

Be an example. You can start today. . .and continue tomorrow.

Thank You for wanting me to be an example, God. I'm not always sure I can be a good one, but when You teach me and then make me brave enough to speak up about it, that means I can share while I keep learning.

DAY 22

SNACKS IN HIDING

[Jesus said,] "The Light has come into the world. And the Light is the test by which men are guilty or not. People love darkness more than the Light because the things they do are sinful."

JOHN 3:19

Snacking is something most people do. You might not be ashamed of it, but some people are. They don't want other people to know they're enjoying something tasty—like potato chips, chocolate bars, or cookies—so they hide when they snack. Maybe they think they'll get in trouble if they're caught. Maybe they're right.

So, where do people snack when they don't want to be seen? The list of secret spots includes their own beds, their cars, a shed, elevators, in the laundry room, the attic, a closet, or maybe a basement.

Maybe you've snacked in one of these places. Maybe you've eaten a snack when you know that you weren't supposed to. Maybe that's why you hid.

People like to hide when they sin. They don't want people to know about their bad choices. They might even think that God won't find out, but He always does.

If we're hiding, that usually means we feel guilty. When we do something wrong, we usually don't want an audience. We will often sin by ourselves, hoping nobody knows or finds out. We might even lie about it if someone asks us. God says this is the normal way for people to respond, but He wants you to be different—He wants you to come to Him. Tell Him what you did. Seek forgiveness. Then? Stay with Him.

God wants any guilt you feel to bring you back to Him. The guilt stays when you don't spend time with God. Unforgiven sin keeps you in the place of guilt. Nobody should want that.

Freedom, however, comes with forgiveness. So come out of hiding and tell God all about whatever makes you feel guilty. You'll not only feel better—you'll be forgiven.

I don't like feeling guilty, Lord. But I am. I've broken Your laws, and I hide when I should come to You. I need You to remind me that coming to You is always my best choice.

DAY 23

DELIVERED ON TIME

Be happy in the Lord. And He will give you the desires of your heart. Give your way over to the Lord. Trust in Him also. And He will do it.

Psalm 37:4–5

Does your family have groceries delivered? If so, you know that the delivery driver usually brings the groceries to your door. Sometimes, the driver leaves the groceries on your porch—a few services might even put them away for you.

What you *don't* expect the driver to do is leave the groceries in the rain on your driveway and then back over them! But that's what happened to an 84-year-old woman in Australia. Thankfully, the grocery store that delivered the food made it clear that this isn't the way they want their groceries to be delivered. So they replaced the food for the customer and said they were sorry.

When God sends you help, it doesn't go to the wrong address, it isn't left in the driveway, and it isn't ruined before you can use it. He knows what you need and who you are. . .and He delivers.

Businesses have customer service departments—places filled with people who try to help customers who've had bad experiences. This job exists because companies know things will go wrong sometimes.

God doesn't need a customer service department. Nothing will ever happen that He doesn't know about. And even when you think something is late, God is at work making sure that whatever you need arrives on time, as long as you've asked Him for help.

It's personal with God. He's aware of everything you ask and everything you say. He doesn't offer anything that He's unwilling to deliver. He gives and keeps on giving, and every one of His gifts is incredible. They may arrive in unusual ways at unusual times, but they will always be a perfect surprise. . . and might just fill you with gratitude.

The things I really need are important to You, Father. Help me remember that what I need and what I simply want are two different things. You meet my needs but might not agree to give me things I want—those things may not be best for me. Help me learn to tell the difference and thank You when You take care of my needs.

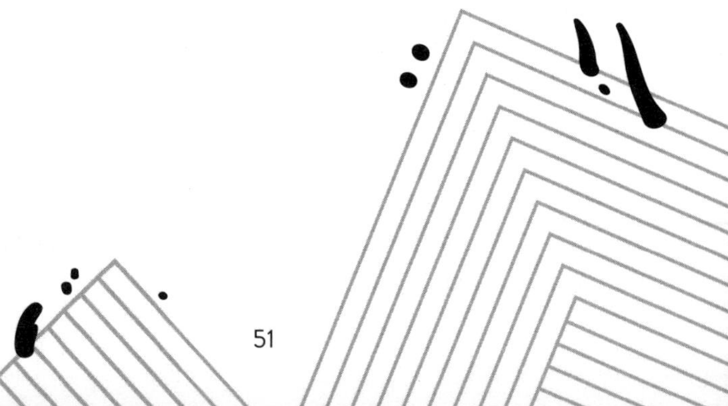

DAY 24

RANGER BETTY AND ABRAHAM

Because Abraham had faith, he obeyed God when God called him to leave his home. He was to go to another country that God promised to give him. He left his home without knowing where he was going.

HEBREWS 11:8

At the age of 84, Betty started her latest career with the National Park Service. She's been known as Ranger Betty for 16 years, and she retired at the age of 100. Betty was the oldest active ranger in California—most people retire 20 years before Betty made up her mind to try something new.

When people came to the historical park in Richmond where Ranger Betty worked, she could tell them stories no one else could. After all, she'd grown up in a time that only she was old enough to remember.

The Bible tells the story of Abraham, who was also given a chance to try something new later in life. While Betty retired at 100, that's the age when Abraham became the father of a baby boy named Isaac. This happened after God told him and his wife, Sarah, to leave the country where they'd always lived—and they obeyed. Talk about an adventure!

God wants you to trust Him too. He doesn't want you to wait until you're 100—He has a plan for you now. And if you live to be 100, He will have a plan for you then, and it will be good.

Every morning when you open your eyes and wonder what you get to do, God already has a plan. You could ignore it, but that would mean giving up an opportunity to do something amazing with a God who designed a perfect day for you. Life doesn't begin when you reach 28, and it doesn't end the day you retire. God made life to be lived every moment you're breathing. Even if you don't have a job, He has something for you to do.

It's easy to think that You wouldn't want to give me an adventure today, God. I'm young and still have a lot of things to learn. But You do incredible things with people of all ages. How old I am is less important to You than whether I'm willing to follow where You lead.

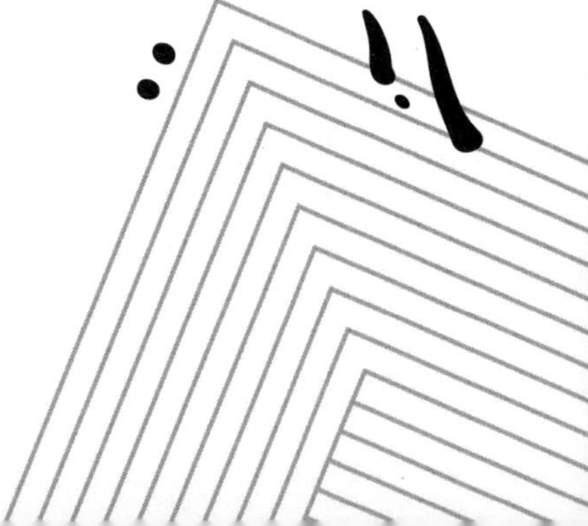

DAY 25

DON'T BE LIZARD LUGGAGE

Be like children who obey. Do not desire to sin like you used to when you did not know any better.
1 PETER 1:14

Two lizards were in the wrong place at the wrong time. . .so they went to the wrong destination. They could have stayed in Florida doing all the lizardy things that lizards do, but they explored a suitcase instead. Curiosity bagged the lizards. While they explored and enjoyed a new experience, the suitcase closed, locking them inside. The owners of the suitcase then took their baggage and went back home to England—which is nowhere near Florida! After 4,000 miles of airplane travel, the lizards bolted from their prison.

It doesn't take much effort to get yourself into trouble. Before you know it, you find yourself in a place you're not supposed to be, but you don't know how to get out and you're not even sure how your experience will end.

Disobedience does that. It takes you from where you should be and makes you a prisoner. You become trapped when you refuse to do what you know you should. Breaking one of God's laws can lead to breaking even more laws, but it doesn't have to be this way. *Don't take that first step.*

God wants you to know that even when you break one of His laws, you should see it as a stop sign. Then, instead of breaking more laws as you run away, you should admit you were wrong and move in His better direction.

Be a boy who obeys. It's never a good idea to be trapped—you know better than that! God didn't make you to be a prisoner, so don't agree to be one. You were made to be free, so make that choice instead. Be free enough to follow God wherever He leads.

Make the best choice today.

I can't follow You perfectly, Lord, and I don't want to pretend that I do. When I break Your law, keep me coming back to You—I don't want to stay where You are not. Give me the courage to admit, the strength to confess, and the bravery to follow You once more.

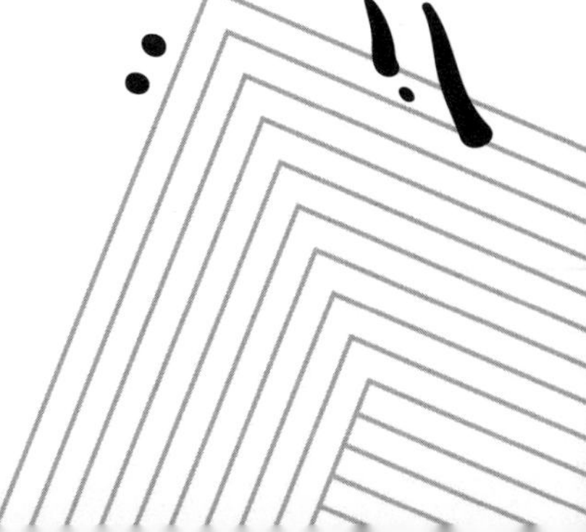

DAY 26

OVERDUE CONFESSION

If we say that we have no sin, we lie to ourselves and the truth is not in us. If we tell Him our sins, He is faithful and we can depend on Him to forgive us of our sins. He will make our lives clean from all sin.

1 John 1:8–9

It takes math skills to figure out how much somebody would owe if a book goes overdue at the library. If the late fee was 14 cents per day, then that adds up to about a dollar after a week. But what happens if someone is nearly 50 years late? Well, you'd need a lot more paper to figure that out! You would take the number of days in the year, multiply that by the number of years, and then multiply again by 14 cents. In the end, the fine for the book would be in the thousands of dollars!

The library at University College London once received a book that had been checked out in 1974. It arrived by mail and included a letter asking the library to treat the book kindly after being away for so long.

Sin can be a lot like a late library book. At first, it might be easy to bring back to God and confess. But when you refuse to do so, it soon grows too large and spirals out of control. Your conscience bothers you, making you feel bad and stealing your joy. God waits to hear from you, but you stay away, hoping He'll forget at some point. But that can only happen once He forgives. So He waits for you to confess what you've done and admit you can't pay the "fine."

He can't show mercy if you won't admit you need it.

I have waited too long to say I'm sorry, Father. I have tried my best to hide, and it doesn't make anything better. I want to accept Your forgiveness, but that will never happen as long as my heart tries to hide something from You. Help me trust You enough to come to You, admit my sins, and then live with a free and forgiven heart.

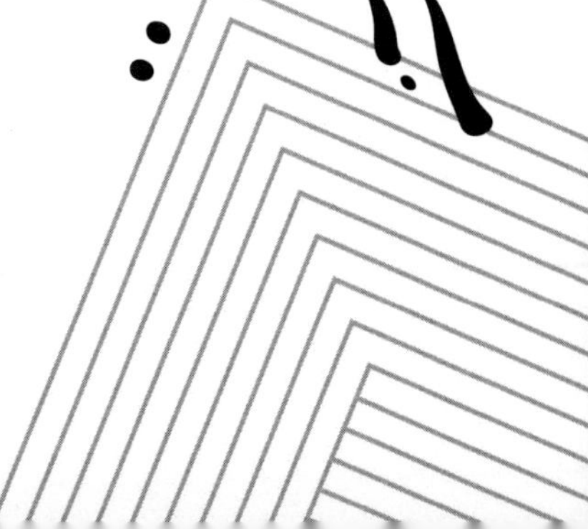

DAY 27

THE GREAT TRANSPLANT

All the Holy Writings are God-given and are made alive by Him. Man is helped when he is taught God's Word. It shows what is wrong. It changes the way of a man's life. It shows him how to be right with God. It gives the man who belongs to God everything he needs to work well for Him.

2 Timothy 3:16–17

A group in Scotland broke a world record by building an insect hotel that's over 7,000 cubic feet—more than twice the size of the previous record holder. This team used spruce trees, bricks, bamboo, wood chips, bark, seeds, and netting to create this "bed and breakfast" for bugs. They cut down trees that weren't supposed to be planted in Scotland and used those trees to create the new home for six-legged critters. What a great way to use "useless" things to make something memorable!

God does that for you. You were made to grow in God's garden, but sin moved you into a place you didn't belong. Staying there never helps you, and everyone around you knows you don't belong there.

When you ask God to place you back in His garden, He will need to trim rotting branches as He moves you home. He can even use what is removed (sin) to help other people avoid sinning.

But you're not a tree—you're a boy. You don't grow in a garden—you grow in God. When you grow, God can use you to help others see that the life He offers will always be better than any other life.

Choose to let God move you to the place where you can grow best. When people learn what you left behind, they might just want to leave their own garden of sin and join you as part of God's family!

Help me grow strong in You, God. Give me all I need to thrive in Your garden. Help me let You remove what will never help me grow so that I can become a healthy Christian with a new purpose. I love You and I need You to help me stay calm when I don't always understand what You're doing. I believe it will be good.

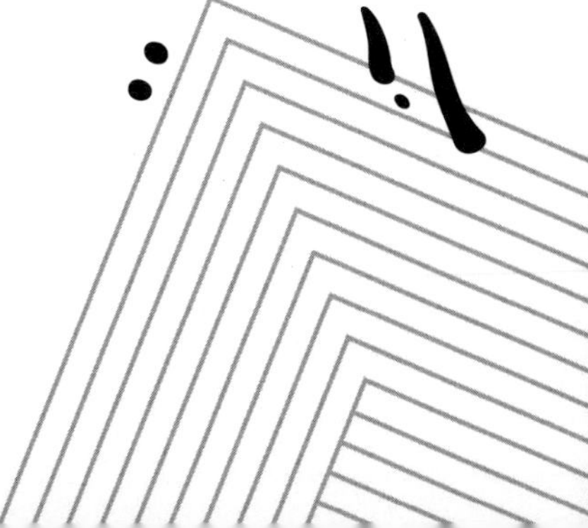

DAY 28

ONE OF A KIND

For You made the parts inside me. You put me together inside my mother. I will give thanks to You, for the greatness of the way I was made brings fear. Your works are great and my soul knows it very well.
Psalm 139:13–14

Maybe you've heard that no two snowflakes are created the same. They're unique and special, yet they can only be clearly seen if they're magnified. And because they melt quickly, most are never explored by a human. But God knows their shape. He created them.

The best humans can do is make a paper snowflake. Those can be pretty unique too. They can also be very large.

College students in Illinois once worked together for more than ten hours to create a paper snowflake nearly 45 feet wide. They took a huge sheet of paper, folded it, and did a lot of cutting to create the massive flake.

The world's largest actual snowflake was 15 inches. But if you witnessed that flake, you'd probably be blown away by God's amazing ability to design. That's important—after all, God made *you*. He created every part of you, making sure you're unique. Your fingerprints are different from anyone else's, even if you have a twin!

Why do you think being different is important? Well, if everyone were exactly alike, the world would be pretty boring, wouldn't it? Everyone would like the same music, so all the songs would sound the same. All the houses would also look alike, and there would only be one type of vehicle.

God made you to love Him and still be one of a kind. You get to bring something to the world that only you can bring. You can do that because God's gift is what makes you unique.

Discover the boy God made you to be, and use your one-of-a-kind life to do something wonderful. God will help you.

Help me stop trying to be like other people, Lord. You didn't create me to be someone else. You made me to be me. May I love You enough to obey You and live my life as someone who is one of a kind.

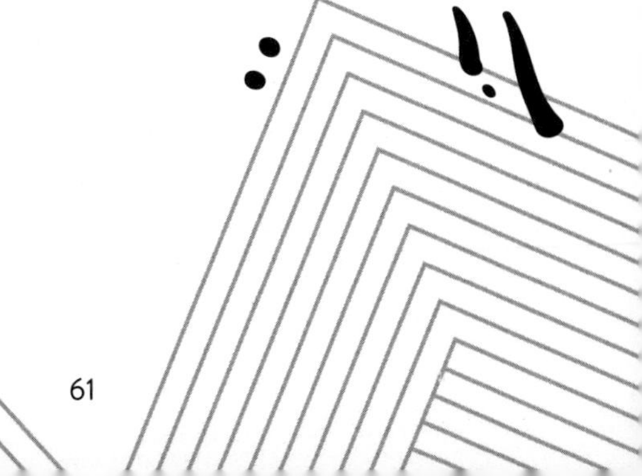

DAY 29

FEARING THE STAGE PROP

Give all your worries to Him because He cares for you.

1 Peter 5:7

Imagine how scary it would be to take a nice stroll one afternoon. . .and stumble across a person's skeleton. Yikes!

Police in Texas once received a call about such a situation, and the caller told them where the bones could be found. The officers arrived and began a serious investigation. But when they were finished (which took less time than you might think) they reached a conclusion: the bones weren't real. What had terrified the caller was just a discarded plastic stage prop skeleton.

Whew!

The things that concern you often turn out to be totally harmless. It's like seeing something in the shadows that makes you think it's horrible, but if you shine a flashlight on it, you might discover it's just a chair.

This is a second reminder that worry does you absolutely no good. Worry takes all the time you're willing to give to it. It demands emotions you don't want to feel. It finds it hilarious that you're willing to keep company with fear.

God never worries. Not even once. He doesn't wonder what tomorrow will be like. He doesn't watch the evening news in surprise. He knows everything that will happen, so nothing is worth worrying about. In fact, He says you should take your fear and let Him toss it out. You don't need it, and He won't keep it.

Maybe you have a few "plastic skeletons" in your life. What you're afraid of may not even be real. God wants you to know the truth and realize that all fear is unimportant.

God cares for you, so He doesn't want any fear—made-up or real—keeping you from spending time with Him.

I've wasted time being afraid, Father. Fear is something I don't want, but I usually accept. I don't know why I forget that You want to take my fear so that I can be free to follow You. Would You help me remember? Would You calm my heart? Would You give me peace? I would be grateful.

DAY 30

TRUST GOD TO RESCUE

Trust in the Lord with all your heart, and do not trust in your own understanding. Agree with Him in all your ways, and He will make your paths straight.

PROVERBS 3:5–6

Alex handles snakes for a living. Usually, these are snakes that no one wants, and he often finds them in unexpected places. So when Alex got a call from a new customer, he got his gear together and headed out. Another day, another unwanted snake.

But Alex could've never expected what happened next.

The caller had discovered a seven-foot-long Vietnamese blue beauty rat snake hiding under a cushion on his couch. You might expect to find the television remote, loose change, or a cell phone there—but certainly not a snake!

The Vietnamese blue beauty rat snake isn't venomous, so it wasn't a real threat to the owner of the couch. But the owner didn't know that. He might not have even believed it. He saw the snake as a threat because the snake looked threatening.

Alex considered it a once-in-a-lifetime snake rescue. The caller just wished it hadn't been in his lifetime—or in his couch.

Sometimes, life can feel like that. You don't expect bad things to happen, you don't want them to, and you can't understand why they happened to you. In those moments, are you trusting God or using your own way of thinking to try to get out of whatever you've gotten into?

God is with you. He protects you. He will guide you. The

worst thing you can do is second guess God's goodness. Instead, trust God to answer your prayer. Even when it seems like you'll need the rescue of a lifetime, trust that He can give it to you!

No need to worry, get upset, or lose perspective—God is good, and He takes care of you.

I'd like to avoid every bad thing, God. But You can teach me how to face hard times and still walk with You toward wherever I need to go. I wouldn't get there on my own because I would give up when things got hard. Train my heart to trust, my mind to believe, and my feet to keep walking with You.

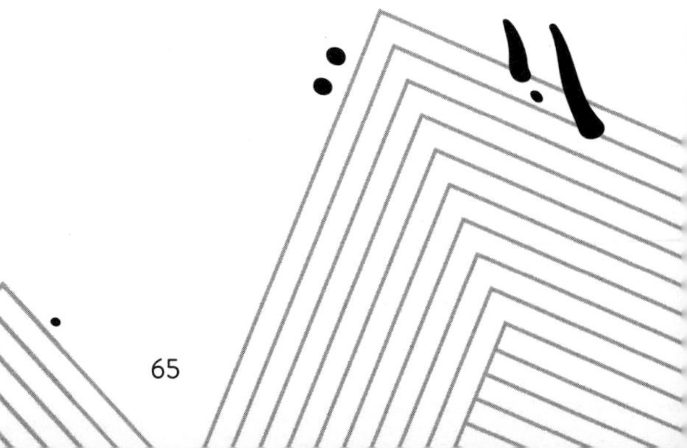

DAY 31

IN PURSUIT OF HONOR

Love each other as Christian brothers.
Show respect for each other.
Romans 12:10

Preston was a boy close to your age when his mom took him to a cemetery to honor his grandpa, who died as a soldier. The gentle wind, rippling flags, and chirping songbirds made the moment memorable. But as Preston's family came prepared to honor his grandpa, the young boy looked around. So many graves were unvisited. *Why?* he wondered.

Then Preston realized he could do something about it. He started a non-profit organization that's raised thousands of dollars to honor veterans. The years continue to pass, and Preston has continued to make honoring fallen soldiers a priority.

What if you decided to show honor to other people? What if you paid attention to the stories that mature people tell? What if you listened to what they did and appreciated the sacrifices they made?

You should honor God first, but you can also remember what others have done to help you. No one was forced to help, but they did anyway. Show them honor, and say thank you with your words and actions.

It never shows honor to believe that people somehow owe you kindness. Their kindness was a gift, and you accepted. You don't have to say thanks, but it shows honor and good manners when you do.

The respect you show to other people both honors them and shows that you're willing to obey God, who asks you to do this. This kind of respect encourages the one you honor, and it can make you see the value in making the good choice.

To honor someone means seeing someone as valuable and treating that person as priceless. Showing honor tells people you think what they've done is important enough for a parade, even if all you can really do is say thanks.

I can—and should—honor You, Lord. There will never be anyone who can do more for me than You already have. But You want me to honor others as well. You want me to throw gossip in the trash and look for the good in what others do. Give me the wisdom to show honor.

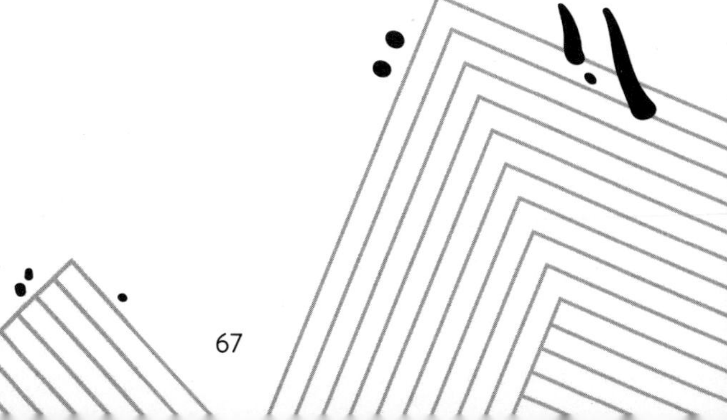

DAY 32

BROCCOLI, THE NOT-SO-GOOD SHEPHERD

[Jesus said,] "I am the Good Shepherd. The Good Shepherd gives His life for the sheep."
JOHN 10:11

He was a donkey named Broccoli. You might not know that donkeys can watch sheep, but apparently, they can. Broccoli, however, might not have been the best "sheep donkey." As soon as the gate was left open, the donkey made a run for it. . . and all the sheep followed! The donkey just wanted to get away from the sheep, and 93 sheep did their best to keep up with him.

The donkey wasn't able to be stealthy—the sheep wouldn't leave him alone. Within an hour, the donkey and all 93 sheep were located. Broccoli went back to work, whether he liked it or not.

Jesus described Christians as sheep. However, He never treats you like an annoyance. He doesn't get angry if you ask questions. He doesn't run whenever it seems like you're distracted. Unlike Broccoli the donkey, Jesus gave His life for people like you. We need someone to follow because we get worried, fearful, and stressed out.

Jesus isn't just called out when no one else is available. He's always on the job, and He's always looking out for those who follow Him.

Of course, that means His sheep should follow Him. They need to go where He leads, stop where He stops, and knock off all that wandering. Sheep get in trouble without a good shepherd. And when sheep grumble, it makes an awful noise that no one appreciates. The sheep have to believe that God will lead and that He knows what He's doing.

The Shepherd is on an adventure, and He continues to encourage sheep to follow Him. Sometimes, sheep need encouragement. Sometimes, they need to be carried. Sometimes, they struggle with obedience. But Jesus isn't running away from you. He'll listen to your complaints and take your fear. He'll make sure you have everything you need to succeed.

His journey will be worth all the trust you can give.

I want—I need—to follow Jesus, Father. Give me feet willing to walk His way and a heart that trusts that His commands are for my good. Help me trust and then obey.

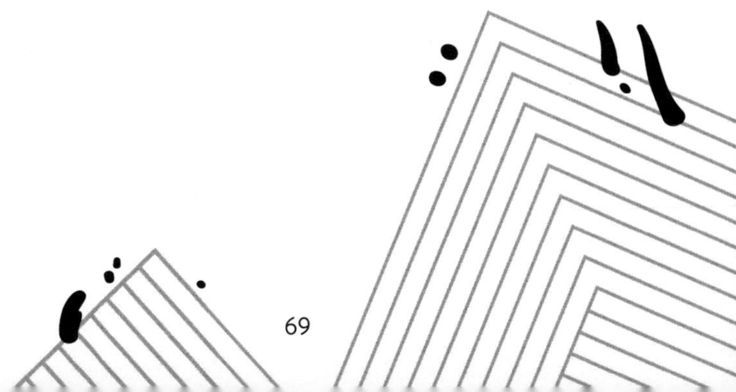

DAY 33

WORLDWIDE WORDS

We have a great Religious Leader Who has made the way for man to go to God. He is Jesus, the Son of God, Who has gone to heaven to be with God. Let us keep our trust in Jesus Christ. Our Religious Leader understands how weak we are. Christ was tempted in every way we are tempted, but He did not sin. Let us go with complete trust to the throne of God. We will receive His loving-kindness and have His loving-favor to help us whenever we need it.

HEBREWS 4:14–16

If you live in England, then you use different words than someone in North America would to describe certain things. In North America, for instance, the covering on an engine is called a "hood"; in England, however, it's called a "bonnet." In North America, the storage compartment of a car is called a "trunk"; in England, it's called a "boot." One continent calls fried potatoes "chips," and England calls them "crisps." Even cookies have another name in England—"biscuits."

This difference in the words we use tells us something about God. While you might not have known the differences between these two regions, God did. He doesn't need a translator. He understands all the languages of earth. Accents aren't an issue. It doesn't even matter if you can't speak. God can hear your thoughts, and He can answer prayers that never reach your lips.

On every continent and in every nation, God is listening. He answers prayers for people who speak every language on earth. Neither skin tones nor locations make God hesitate to help—His love is without borders.

God knows what you're saying because He speaks the language of the human heart. Communication with Him has no roadblocks. . .except the ones you put up. Don't ever believe God wouldn't listen to you. Explain yourself all you want, but God still understands, loves, and shows kindness to people—no matter where they live on the map.

I sometimes say things that other people don't understand. But You do, God. Thanks for understanding even when others are confused. Thanks for listening even when I don't know the words to say. Thanks for listening even when the words I use are different from the ones others use. Thanks for loving me enough to pay attention.

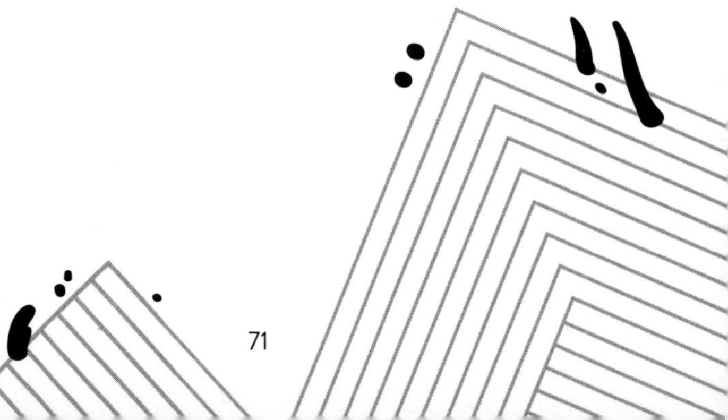

DAY 34

NEW LIFE—NEW CHOICES

If a man belongs to Christ, he is a new person. The old life is gone. New life has begun.

2 CORINTHIANS 5:17

Have you ever gone snow skiing? Learning to ski often involves taking classes—there's a whole new set of words, objects, and techniques you need to memorize. Sometimes, skiers call mountains "hills." Bumps in the snow are called "moguls." If you need to slow down, you do something called "snowplow."

Skis have made room for snowboards, and they sometimes make room for a strange vehicle—one that looks a bit like a motorless snowmobile crossed with a bicycle. To drive this thing, you sit and use handlebars to move the front ski. There are two more skis side by side in the back. Those who use this device say this "ski bike" is easier to learn than skiing itself!

Sometimes, new things can be confusing and really hard to get used to. You might not like the idea of giving up your old way of doing something so that you can learn to do it a new way. But that's just what God needs you to do. His plans for your life look a little different than the way most people live.

You might look for a way to get back at someone who's been mean to you, but God says the new way is to forgive. You might think it's okay to dislike some people and like others, but God wants you to love *all* people. You might think you must try to be important, but God wants you to treat other people like they're more important.

Following God means learning how to do things in a new

way. Not only will you learn, but God will also want you to do something with what you learn. When you know what He wants, you can do what He asks. When you do what He asks, you show Him that you can be trusted with even bigger things.

Obedience means greater adventure with God!

I want Your greatest adventure, Lord. Help me choose to obey so that I can do new things with You. I want this new life to make sense. Help me learn what I need to know so that I can do what You need me to do.

DAY 35

FAST-TRACKED FAITH

Do your best to know that God is pleased with you. Be as a workman who has nothing to be ashamed of. Teach the words of truth in the right way.
2 TIMOTHY 2:15

For many boys, school is not easy—at least the classes in which you have to follow a textbook. You may do all the practice drills and homework sheets yet still struggle to remember the answer to question five on a test.

A 12-year-old boy named Deep had a different problem. Nothing seemed to be a challenge for him. In first grade, he was reading at a seventh-grade level. He breezed through several grades early and then went on to college before he turned 13. At this rate, he could finish college before he could get a driver's license!

Learning can seem hard. The things you need to remember can be very easy to forget. That's why God teaches you what you need to know and helps you remember what you've learned. The real question is whether or not you want to learn. If you don't know for sure, then the answer is probably no. That makes God sad. He wants you to have the best life possible, and that means learning things that only He can teach. You'll need to pay attention. Waiting until you're an adult will only waste time that could be used to learn more about God.

When you learn something from God, He's ready to teach you more. But if you decide you don't want to believe what you're learning, then you may need to stay on that lesson until you discover the value of what God's trying to teach.

You can put your journey with God on a fast track. You don't have to drag your feet, pretend that it doesn't matter, or ignore your assignments.

Remember: God is teaching. . .and you can be learning.

I have been guilty of not really wanting to learn more about You sometimes, Father. But You don't want me to feel this way. You have so many things to teach me, so help me learn. Help me remember. Help me share what I learn too—it will be the best news someone else will ever hear.

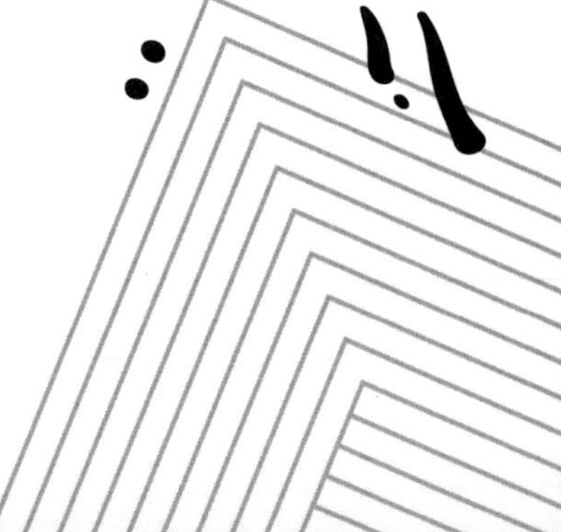

DAY 36
GIVE BECAUSE HE GAVE

Remember, the man who plants only a few seeds will not have much grain to gather. The man who plants many seeds will have much grain to gather. Each man should give as he has decided in his heart. He should not give, wishing he could keep it. Or he should not give if he feels he has to give. God loves a man who gives because he wants to give.
2 Corinthians 9:6–7

Sam drives a compact automobile, and he doesn't live much differently than he did in college. However, by the time he was 30, Sam owned a successful company and made millions of dollars each year. Most people might wish they made this kind of money. . .and Sam doesn't plan to ever stop increasing his paycheck.

But if Sam makes so much money, why does he still live like he did when he was in college? Because Sam gives away 99 percent of every dollar he earns.

When he was in college, Sam figured out that giving really is something worth doing. You can find this wisdom in the Bible. Everything you'll ever receive is ultimately a gift from God. He wants you to share what He's given. He wants you to take care of your gifts and use them to help others too. If you can remember that God will use your belongings to answer other people's prayers, then it might be a little easier to share with someone in need.

God says that when His followers are faithful in taking care of what He gives them, they shouldn't be surprised when He trusts them with more. He does this so that they may be an even greater blessing to others. That's hard to do when His people won't share.

Your future job may be very different from Sam's. You may not be able to give millions of dollars. God, however, is happy to see you start where you are. That's how He checks out your faithfulness.

I want to be faithful in giving what You share with me, God. Help me see that nothing really belongs to me—it's all a tool that You can use to bless others. Give me the wisdom to share well.

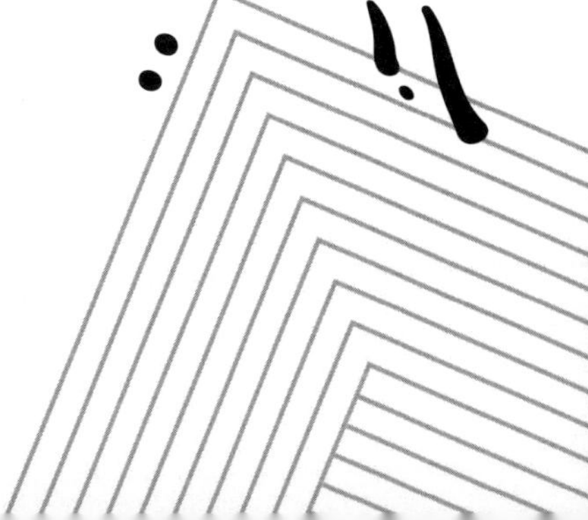

DAY 37

BE A REAL POTATO

Do not act like the sinful people of the world. Let God change your life. First of all, let Him give you a new mind. Then you will know what God wants you to do. And the things you do will be good and pleasing and perfect.

ROMANS 12:2

If you've ever visited a potato cellar, you know there's a unique odor. Potatoes grow in the ground, so they smell a little earthy. If you worked in a potato factory, however, you'd probably get used to the smell. As the potatoes roll down the line, it might be your job to watch for any bits of mud, debris, or other items that don't belong.

That's what happened at a factory in New Zealand. One staff member noticed something a bit unusual about a potato and pulled it from the line. The worker wiped the mud away. . .and then called the bomb squad! This was no oddly shaped potato—it was a grenade from World War II!

After x-raying the grenade, the bomb squad discovered that it had been used for training. There were no explosives inside (thankfully!) because the grenade's deadly contents had been removed.

Don't settle for being a broken grenade in a world of potatoes. In other words, don't try to act like you love God when you don't. This confuses people. Instead, learn to love God with every part of you (heart, mind, soul, and spirit). God doesn't want pretenders. If you want God to change your life, then let Him do it. If you want a new mind, then let Him give you one. Learn what God wants you to do—the last thing He wants is someone who lies about who he is.

Be as real as God makes you. Be as honest as He is. Be as authentic as someone with new life.

It seems easy to pretend, Lord. I can act one way around Christian friends and a different way around people who don't think You're very important. When I choose to follow You, help me look like someone who follows You. Help me recognize Your wisdom, show Your kindness, and never be ashamed that I know You.

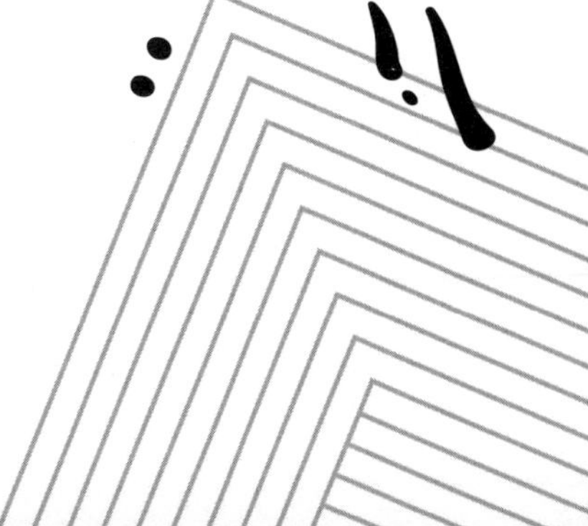

DAY 38

WALKING WITH A FRIEND

A friend loves at all times. A brother is born to share troubles.
Proverbs 17:17

Being on horseback is all in a day's work for David. He used to ride bulls, so a horse is no big deal. But maybe David has gone a little soft since retirement. He lives about six miles from town, but at least once a week, he puts a saddle on his horse, Jackson, and they head to town. Does he need supplies? No. Does he need to attend an important meeting? Not really. David rides his horse to town to get a cup of coffee for himself and a donut hole for Jackson.

A horse may not be a perfect replacement for human friendship, but David and Jackson still look out for each other. In this case, David gets a ride to town while Jackson gets a fried piece of dough. Both seem to like how things turn out.

God made friendships very important. After all, He made sure you could be friends with Him—and that should always be your best friendship.

You can also be friends with members of your family, neighbors, and classmates. You should choose your friends carefully—only the good ones will encourage you to keep walking with God. These friends can help when you need help, encourage you when you need encouragement, and walk with you when you feel like stopping.

There's hope in friendship. It means that whatever you're going through, you don't have to go through it alone. Friends listen and then pray to the God who listens. They walk with you and walk with the God who gave you a journey. These friends stick around, even when things are really hard. That definitely describes God, but it might also describe someone else you know.

Walk with friends, talk with friends, and choose to be a friend. You'll need good ones—so be a good one yourself!

Thank You for being my friend, Father. I want to know how to be the type of friend that You've been to me. Help me find good friends, be a good friend, and value friendship as much as You do.

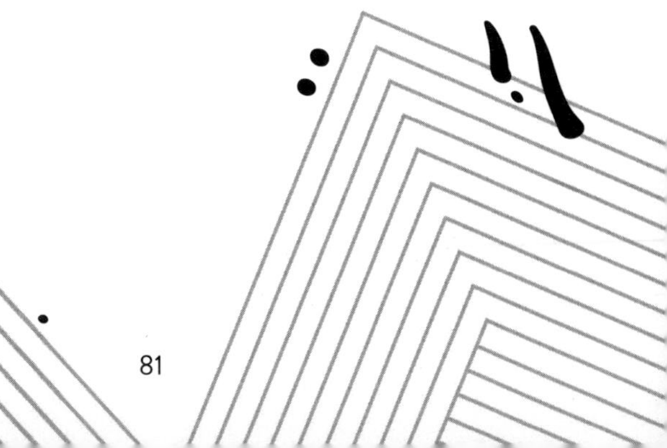

DAY 39

FOLLOW THE LEADER

I will show you and teach you in the way you should go. I will tell you what to do with My eye upon you.
PSALM 32:8

It's not clear if the driver was using GPS, but he definitely made a wrong turn.

Firefighters in Maine were called to help a man who tried (and failed) to navigate through a garbage dump. Somehow, he found his car caught over a massive trash compactor. The driver couldn't get out, so first responders came to the rescue. The good news is that the driver wasn't injured, and a towing company was able to rescue the damaged car so that it didn't end up in the trash.

It's easy to get lost, isn't it? You can make plans but then get distracted somewhere along the way. You can do the same thing with God. He has good, easy-to-understand directions, but you need to follow.

You have a choice: follow Him or blaze your own trail. And if you don't know where you're going, your trailblazing will probably be wild and unsuccessful. Soon, you'll end up at the wrong destination in a load of trouble. Thankfully, you can avoid this if you do things the way God says they should be done.

It doesn't make sense to follow people who don't follow God. They're just guessing. They might think they know what's good for you, but often, the way God does things is really different from anyone else's way. If anyone can give good directions, it's God.

There will come days when you might think you're doing what God wants, but if it's not what He says in the Bible, then you're not really following God. This is what the Bible calls "deceiving yourself." That means you believe a lie that *you* told.

Talk about being confused!

Always remember that God is never confused. He knows the truth, shares the truth, and says this truth will set you free.

Following the leader is an easy decision if that leader is You, God. I don't want to keep being guilty of trying to figure out what to do. I have questions, which is great because You have answers. Help me learn as I follow.

DAY 40

LOOK DIFFERENT

Prove yourselves to be without blame. . . .
Shine as lights among the sinful people of this world.
PHILIPPIANS 2:15

Alex's car won't break any speed records, but he doesn't mind. The car can only reach 23 miles per hour on the best of days. At 39 inches wide, 39 inches tall, and 53 inches long, it's the world's smallest car—its gas tank holds just over a gallon of fuel. (This also means that Alex has the lowest fuel bill in Britain!)

Alex saw this car on television and eventually found a replica he could afford. It's become his favorite vehicle to drive as he manages his daily chores around his village. Alex likes owning a car very few people have ever seen. Lots of people take notice and ask him questions about his peculiar little car.

Your Christian life is a bit like Alex's car. To some people, it seems small, useless, and odd. But the Christian life takes you places, it fits you, and it gets people talking.

But that's where the similarities end. Unlike a car, your Christian life is active and living. It changes people's lives and futures. It makes the impossible possible.

It's hard to compare the Christian life to anything because it's different than everything else. Some examples are closer than others, but you can learn the most about the Christian life by reading the Bible—and books like this one. You grow whenever you live out what you learn and have a thirst to know more.

You may be small like the car Alex drives, but with God,

you can be brave, mighty, and bold. God gives you everything you need to live the life He knows you can live. If you don't live the Christian life, it will never be because God let you down.

Accept His help to accomplish what you can only do with His help.

You're always strong, Lord, even when I'm weak. I can't do what You do, but You can make me strong enough to do what You want me to do. I grow with You, and I can do amazing things when You're by my side.

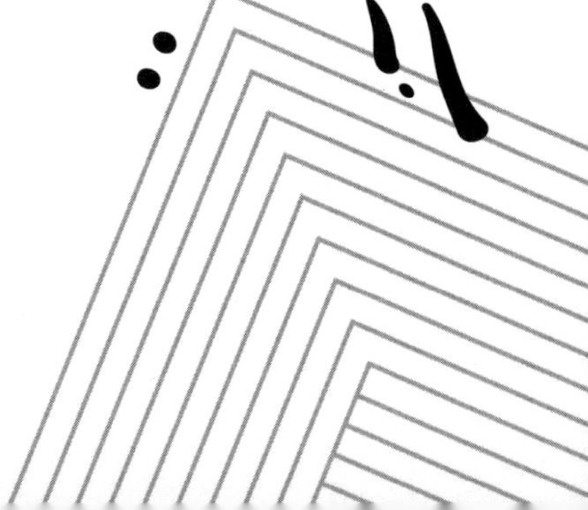

DAY 41

SERVE—DON'T STEAL

Anyone who steals must stop it! He must work with his hands so he will have what he needs and can give to those who need help.
EPHESIANS 4:28

Pompeii is a famous city in Italy. It was destroyed when the nearby Mount Vesuvius volcano erupted nearly 2,000 years ago. Much of the city still exists—it's just buried under ash and cooled lava.

This old city has become a great place for treasure seeking—for both scientists and criminals. Some people sneak in and steal artifacts to sell to the highest bidder, despite all those who want the archeological site to stay protected.

But now, any artifact thief who comes to Pompeii has to bypass an unexpected obstacle: a pair of robotic dogs. These robots look for safety issues—such as if one of the buildings is about to fall—and let scientists know about them. People who come to steal would probably be pretty scared if they spotted one of those robot dogs!

Pompeii is not always a safe place to be, but it's also not something that scientists want to lose. That's why they use robots—to prevent Pompeii from being destroyed.

God gives wonderful gifts like love, life, forgiveness, and hope. You can accept what He gives, but don't try to steal what He shares. If something belongs to someone else, don't try taking it. God's children don't work to earn His free gifts—they work to show they're serious about taking care of their family and people in need.

God wants you to help others, and this help requires you to do something. It takes effort. It's more than wishing someone well or sending up a quick prayer. You should do these things, of course, but you should also help if you can. That's how you can give someone the same type of gift that God gave you.

There's no good reason to destroy the example that God gave you to follow.

Doing work well is just what You do, Father. You can help me—You've done this before. Give me the energy, wisdom, and willingness to work to help others too.

DAY 42

SQUID CERTIFIED HOT

All You know is too great for me. It is too much for me to understand.
Psalm 139:6

You might not drink coffee or tea, but you've probably had a cup of hot cocoa. If so, you know how important it is to store the drink in a container that keeps it hot—it just doesn't taste right if you don't.

But how does that work? Well, scientists got the idea by studying the things God made. For instance, scientists discovered that the skin of a squid helps with maintaining a constant temperature—it keeps cold things cold and hot things hot. Scientists wouldn't actually use a squid's skin, but they can take what they learn and make something that imitates what God already did.

Because God knows everything, He knew before He made a squid that this information would one day come in handy for us. The thrill we find in discovering something like this might just make God happy. He always has a reason for the things He does, even though it sometimes takes a very long time for anyone to notice.

Long ago, nobody had lightbulbs. . .and then we did. There didn't use to be any phones; now, almost everyone carries one. In the past, cars didn't exist; today, some can drive themselves.

You can learn new things that God always knew. What seems miraculous to you is common knowledge to God. Do you think God is pleased when people find creative ways to use His creation? Of course! Does He ever wonder why it took them so long to figure it out? Probably not. Remember: God knows everything, so He always knew how long it'd take for someone to notice His surprises.

God finds joy when humans get excited over helpful new discoveries. That's just what God has always wanted. Sharing new discoveries means that people will want to know more about the God who made it all—even squid skin!

It can be easy to stop being impressed when so many new things come along, God. Help me remember that everything new would never be possible without something You made first. Maybe that will change the way I think about all these new things so that I can see You as amazing.

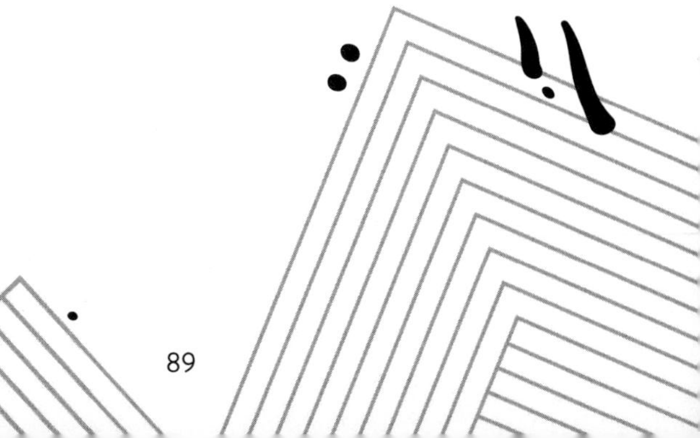

DAY 43

THE CULPRIT

"The robber comes only to steal and to kill and to destroy. I came so they might have life, a great full life."
John 10:10

The mystery happened at Christine's house. First, one toy disappeared and then another. It seemed like her daughter's toys were vanishing every day. Christine looked everywhere she could think of, but she still found no evidence of the missing toys. This mom then set up cameras to see who or what was taking the toys. Soon, she learned the secret—their pet cat would pick a toy when no one was around and then hide it. After seeing the video, Christine was able to reclaim the cat's stolen treasure and restore it to the little girl. And now this mom keeps a close eye on a certain toy-stealing feline.

God has an enemy, and this enemy wants to see you fail. He spends time paying attention to what you like and dislike. He wants to steal your things and convince you that it's fun to break God's rules. This enemy never stops lying to you. He tries to make you feel good about making bad choices—but when you finally give in and do something bad, he'll scream that you're a horrible person. He wants you to believe that God could never love someone like you.

This robber/thief/liar is only interested in seeing you destroyed. No encouragement he offers is real. He hates anyone who loves God. He pretends to like you just so you will let him get close enough to destroy you.

This is the truth about Satan. Like Christine's cat, he steals what's yours and hides your joy. He never admits he did anything to you.

But don't be frightened. God is bigger than this enemy. God will encourage and love you. God will forgive, not condemn. He does good things that Satan will never do. God will never tell you that you're a failure. He wants you to succeed.

So which will it be? God. . .or God's enemy? It's your choice. Be careful.

You can help me recognize the work of Your enemy, Lord. You want the best for me, but Satan never will. You want me to learn from You, but the devil wants me to be confused. I need to recognize the difference—and then follow You.

DAY 44

THE WORK YOU DO

Whatever work you do, do it with all your heart. Do it for the Lord and not for men. Remember that you will get your reward from the Lord. He will give you what you should receive. You are working for the Lord Christ.

Colossians 3:23–24

Every year, members of a British charity look for a little help. No, it's not serving meals to the homeless or gathering clothes for the needy. They're looking for someone to run a post office. Strange, right? But this isn't an ordinary post office—it's in Antarctica!

When they find someone they like, they keep that person at the cold outpost from November through March (that's summer in Antarctica). People with this job are always busy—when they aren't making sure the mail is ready, they're out counting penguins! The post office has limited electricity, there's no running water, and internet access is unavailable.

What if someone asked you to do this job? Would you take it? What if someone asked you to do another job you don't like?

It is great when you really like a job, but sometimes you're asked to do things at home that you don't like. What kind of attitude do you have when you have to do something you don't enjoy? You might make sure other people know you're not happy. You might refuse to do the job. You might get angry.

God, however, wants you to put the same amount of effort into whatever you do, whether you love it or hate it. When you take out the trash, you should treat it as if God asked you to do it. When you make your bed, think about how much effort you'd put into it if you knew God would be checking your work. When you have homework or Mom asks you to help in the kitchen, be willing, because God loves seeing you do your best.

It seems like there's always something to do, Father. But if I feel this way, I can't imagine how You must feel. Not a moment goes by where You aren't doing something good for someone. Help me be willing to obey my parents and teachers with a good attitude. I want to do my work well.

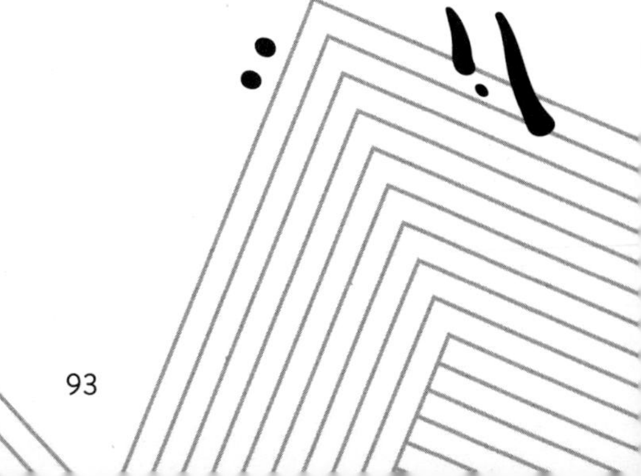

DAY 45

WHAT ARE YOU CHASING?

We are Christ's missionaries. God is speaking to you through us. We are speaking for Christ and we ask you from our hearts to turn from your sins and come to God.
2 Corinthians 5:20

Alligators have big teeth and strong jaws. They might frighten you, especially when you don't know where they are in the water. In Florida, however, there was one alligator that made people smile. Someone operated a remote-controlled toy boat in a local pond, and the alligator chased it wherever it went. No one knows if the alligator thought the boat was food or if it just wanted to play.

You might chase things that aren't very helpful too. Perhaps you chase gossip and leave compassion behind. Maybe you chase lies and stop looking for truth. You might even run after something you think you might enjoy more than learning from God.

When Christians refuse to follow God or obey His law, they need forgiveness. They also need to change how they do things.

There are a lot of things you can chase, but just like the alligator, you won't be fed. Chasing after these things will never make you grow. It might be fun for a while, but you'll still be hungry at the end. And each new day, you get to choose whether to chase God (who *will* satisfy your hunger for important things) or something that's bright and shiny but not worth chasing. Those other things—a high score, a new trading card, some unique skill, and so on—might be impressive, but they're often useless.

When you feel like chasing something, ask yourself if what you're chasing will bring you closer to God or farther away from Him. Are you chasing it to love others more or to prove you're better than others? When you chase something that isn't God, does it make it easier or harder to obey His rules?

I don't want to waste time chasing things that never leave me satisfied, God. I could do that every day if I don't accept Your help. Give me good things to chase that help me get closer to You. I love You and I'm thankful You want me to find You.

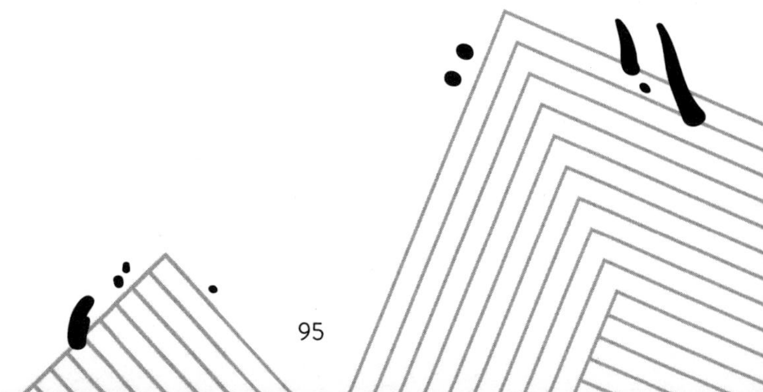

DAY 46

ROMAN'S KINDNESS

What if a person has enough money to live on and sees his brother in need of food and clothing? If he does not help him, how can the love of God be in him? My children, let us not love with words or in talk only. Let us love by what we do and in truth.

1 John 3:17–18

Roman was just a boy when his family took care of a little puppy named Maggie. She was too young to be adopted, but she needed help. Roman learned to love Maggie very quickly. He described her as the best dog. But Maggie wouldn't be around forever—a new and permanent family would soon adopt Maggie, and the boy knew a goodbye would be coming.

It was still hard, but Roman decided he could write letters to Maggie's new family. The letters told them all about his experiences with Maggie and how one dog in need brought out the kindness in this boy's heart.

People will remember your kindness. It grows trust, invites friendship, and inspires love. It's easy to be mean, but being mean doesn't help anyone. Being kind may be a little harder, but it helps everyone. It's exactly what God wants you to do. Kind is what God wants you to be—after all, it's what He's always been to you.

Your kindness might be a one-time event for someone you meet. You might never see that person again, yet simply smiling or holding the door could brighten someone's day. In other cases, you might be around people who need kindness every day. . .so that's what you should do. Kindness isn't just a free sample—God wants it to come naturally for His children.

What if God could use *your* kindness to help someone recognize His own? What if someone wanted to learn more? What if that learning could change someone's life? The possibilities are endless—and they all start with kindness.

Kindness isn't just something I do when I feel like it, Lord. I'm thankful that Your kindness, love, and forgiveness don't just change with the weather—they're constant. If You always show kindness, then why shouldn't I? Help me make kindness the normal way I treat people.

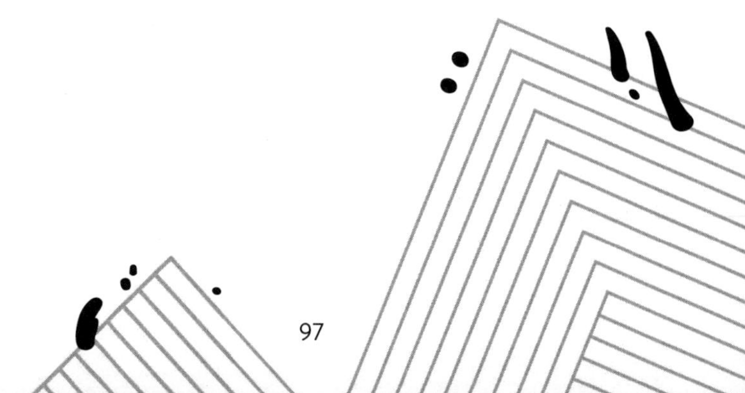

DAY 47

A SATISFYING RESULT

Give your way over to the Lord.
Trust in Him also. And He will do it.
Psalm 37:5

Colin knows how to keep himself busy—and for him, that often means using a shovel. While he had never attempted to build a tunnel, he suddenly decided to move 7,000 pounds of dirt each day, creating a tunnel large enough to let him stand up straight and walk from his house to his shed (forty feet away). The reason? So that he wouldn't have to get wet going outside.

The tunnel is sturdy, so it does exactly what he wanted it to do. Colin's very satisfied with the result. He shared the journey on social media, and more than six million people watched his progress. Some even wished they had a tunnel like the one Colin built.

When you follow God, you might feel a little like Colin. You're doing something you've never done, going somewhere you've never been, and trusting that the one you're following has more answers than you have questions. The journey seems too big, and you're not sure you'll reach the end. At times, you have no idea what you're even doing.

But other people may be watching to see how you handle your journey, and they see things that make them wish they had what you have. Stick with it long enough, and you'll see God accomplish things you know you could never do on your own. He steps into your "I just can't do it" moment and says, "That's true, you can't. But *I* can."

You can be satisfied if you trust God enough to do things that don't always make sense. When you obey God, you're saying that you trust Him. This is called faith. God created the path you walk, so there's nothing in your journey that He doesn't already know. This path provides protection, companionship, and instruction. God knows you can do it, and He makes sure you have enough room to get to Him from here.

Give me the ability to endure the biggest journey of my life, Father. Help me see where I should take my next step. Give me enough wisdom to want to be with You—now and always. I'm doing something big because You made it amazing. Keep leading—I'll keep watching and walking.

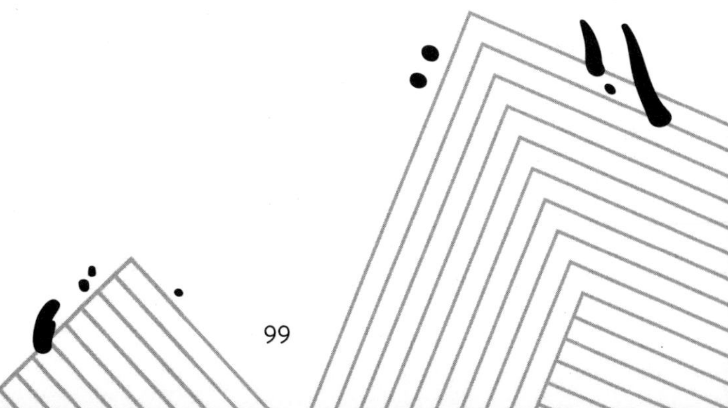

DAY 48

THE GOOD PILLOWS

We know that God makes all things work together for the good of those who love Him and are chosen to be a part of His plan. God knew from the beginning who would put their trust in Him. So He chose them and made them to be like His Son. Christ was first and all those who belong to God are His brothers.

ROMANS 8:28–29

Buford had been married for nearly 70 years when his wife died. They'd done so many things together, and he missed her very much. But Buford found a way to honor his wife's memory—he took up volunteering.

He chose to do something his wife had always done: sewing. She had made pillows for the homeless in their old Kentucky home. Now Buford would make pillows.

Buford is honoring his wife's memory, and by doing so, he's helping his community. When Buford sews, he gives—but the activity is also a way for him to remember his wife.

It's possible to be so sad that you miss something special God may want you to do. You might think so much about the bad that you miss the good that God wants you to notice. God wants His joy to last longer than your sorrow. Please remember that God can use even life's worst moments to make all things new.

The hardest moments may have a softened ending. Tragedy can lead to joy. God can reward your patience with the joy of knowing that everything will be alright.

Buford would be very happy if his wife were still alive, but plenty of people now get a better night's sleep because his wife taught him how to do something helpful. His bad situation brought good to someone else. In helping others, Buford has discovered a good outcome.

What a great lesson we all can learn!

I wouldn't want to face the future if I dwelled on the bad things that might happen, God. If I think about it too much, I begin to worry, and then I'm not helpful to anyone. Instead, I want You to use me to answer other people's prayers. The help I can offer might be just what someone needs right now. Help everyone see something good come from my bad experiences. Help people say thanks.

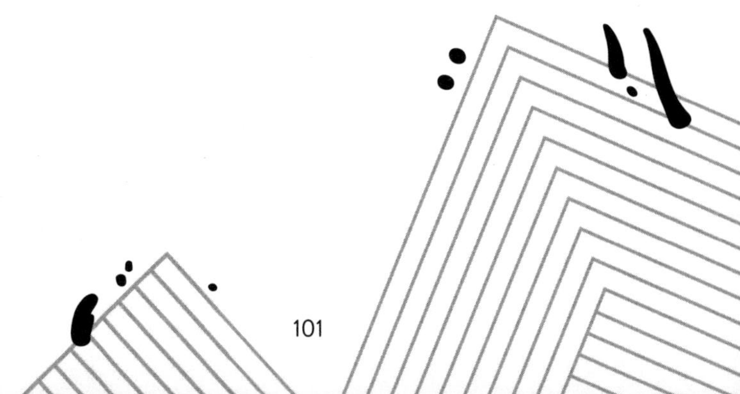

DAY 49

COMFORT LIKE A PUPPY

[God] gives us comfort in all our troubles. Then we can comfort other people who have the same troubles. We give the same kind of comfort God gives us.
2 CORINTHIANS 1:4

Kids find comfort in different things. It might be a blanket, toy, or something they received as a gift and that they now carry in their pocket. Whatever it is, they just can't live without it. For four-year-old Leo, the thing that comforts him is a stuffed puppy, which he simply named Puppy. Puppy goes everywhere with Leo—at least most of the time. Once, Leo sat the toy down because he was distracted. He was still distracted when he accidentally left Puppy behind.

Leo's mom posted a picture of Puppy on social media to see if anyone had found the beloved toy. No one had. However, another mom, who knew how important a toy like Puppy was to a boy, remembered that she had the exact same toy at home. Her kids didn't play with it—maybe Leo would be happy with a substitute. He was.

No matter how old you are, you'll have days when you need to be comforted. God knows that, and He also knows other people need comfort too. So He comforts you and then wants you to use His kindness to comfort others.

There are two big words to describe this kind of comfort: *sympathy* and *empathy*. Sympathy means you've struggled in the same way other people struggle, so you have a pretty good idea how hard things are for them. Empathy means you don't have any idea of what people have been through because it's never happened to you, but you believe they are hurting, so you want them to know you're sad with them.

God calls this comfort by many other names: *kindness*, *patience*, *love*, and *compassion* are just a few. He wants you to care enough about people that they recognize the gift of comfort and are grateful God sent you to help.

I want people to see Your compassion in the way I choose to help, Lord. Help me reassure hurting people that, with You, everything will be alright.

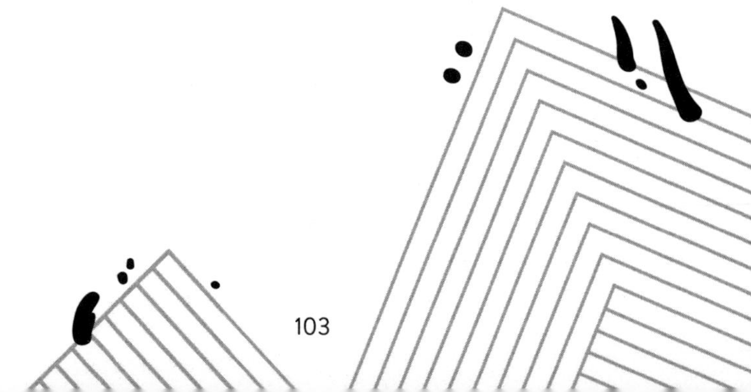

DAY 50

SEE IT—DO IT

If you know what is right to do but you do not do it, you sin.
JAMES 4:17

Kana and her younger sister, Kaning, were enjoying the outdoors at their family's home in Thailand. Suddenly, something terrible happened: Kaning fell into the four-foot-deep pool in their yard. As Kaning struggled to keep her head above water, Kana called out to her father. Her dad didn't hesitate—he immediately plunged in to save his daughter.

Heroes do that kind of thing. And every day, new heroes show up. They take *initiative*, which means they look for what needs to be done and they do it—no questions asked and no worrying about whether they have enough time or training. They just step in and help.

You get to do that too. You'll likely never need permission to clean the table, take out the trash, or make your bed. If you see something that needs to be done and then just do it, it will make quite an impression. Your family will notice, and they'll appreciate it.

Such actions are the fruit God is trying to grow in your life: "The fruit that comes from having the Holy Spirit in our lives is: love, joy, peace, not giving up, being kind, being good, having faith, being gentle, and being the boss over our own desires. The Law is not against these things" (Galatians 5:22–23).

Imagine if something embarrassing happens to someone. What will you do—laugh or help? Which response will everyone remember positively? If someone is hurt, will you act like you don't notice, or will you lend a hand? Which response has the best chance of ending in friendship? Someone needs help in the yard. Will you help or just wave as you walk by to go spend time with friends? Which response seems like something a good neighbor would do?

The word of the day is *initiative*. If you see a need, meet a need—there's no time to waste!

I want to show initiative, Father. Grow Your fruit in my life, and when it's full grown, let things like love, joy, and kindness show up and help out. May I do what is right because it's always the right thing to do.

DAY 51

THE VOICE

[Jesus said,] "My sheep hear My voice and I know them. They follow Me."
JOHN 10:27

Maria does what most college students do. She goes to college and then works a part-time job to pay for her education. In Maria's case, she bags groceries at a store in Texas. One day, while the carts made their wobbly-wheel noise and the scanner beeped, Maria noticed a woman in line with two boys. When it came time for the woman to pay, she didn't have enough money. *I can't help her*, Maria thought, but something kept telling her to take care of the rest. She did. The woman, it turns out, was the grandmother of the boys, and she was working hard to take care of them—the only other option was to place them in a foster home.

What was it that kept telling Maria to help? The answer is God. God's voice may not sound like a voice you'd hear other people use. It may be quiet. It could be a thought that won't leave. It could be something you read in the Bible. People have heard God's voice in these ways for a very long time.

Christians learn to recognize God's voice so that they can do things they might never do otherwise. God's voice will lead people to show His love to others—just like Maria did to the grandmother.

Dare to help when God whispers that there's a need. You don't have to know how or why the need arose—all you have to do is be willing to listen, knowing that God will use your actions to help others.

You pray, and God listens. Other people pray, and God listens to them too. You can also listen, and when you do, He might just link your ears to His voice. So if you hear that deep down, whispered voice of God, it's a good idea to pay attention.

I want to recognize Your voice, God. You might have something important for me to do, and I don't want to miss it because I was listening to something else. Give me good ears to hear You.

DAY 52

GIDDY GIVING

God can give you all you need. He will give you more than enough. You will have everything you need for yourselves. And you will have enough left over to give when there is a need.

2 Corinthians 9:8

Isaac had big plans for his 14th birthday—plans that involved a party and lots of friends. There would be cake, noise, laughter, and mayhem. Pretty normal party, right? But one thing would be very different: these friends weren't going to buy Isaac anything.

This is just what the birthday boy wanted. He asked them each to bring at least five dollars. They would then take all the money to the store and buy toys for a local charity in their home state of Idaho.

Some people might have wondered about a bunch of kids walking through the store and buying things, but that didn't stop Isaac's friends. They surprised a group of kids who weren't expecting a gift, especially since it wasn't *their* birthday!

God loves it when people of all sizes are cheerful about giving. These kinds of people don't give while secretly wishing they didn't have to.

Giving cheerfully shows love for other people and puts their needs above your own. And since God makes it a priority to love and help, He sets the perfect example. Follow Him. Share like He shares. Love like He loves.

Isaac didn't have to give on a day when everyone expected

him to receive gifts, but he did anyway. And because of his kindness, this was probably one of the most memorable birthdays he ever had. There were enough blessings for everyone.

Let Isaac's story inspire you to do something brave and memorable—something that includes a great deal of giddy.

Is it okay to admit I'm sometimes afraid to give, Lord? If I give what I have, then I won't have enough to buy things I want. That sounds selfish, but it's how I feel sometimes. Help me understand how good it can be to give and how much it can bless other people. I want to remember the experience of blessing others for the rest of my life.

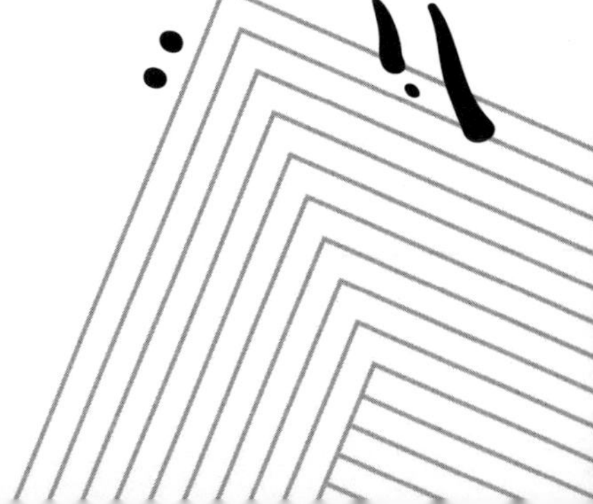

DAY 53

A BRAND-NEW FOREST

Let us help each other to love others and to do good.
HEBREWS 10:24

Hakmet is a 78-year-old man who lives near the Black Sea. He could have retired, but he has a job to do. Sometime after his 50th birthday, Hakmet had an idea: he wanted to turn nearly 25,000 acres of barren hills into a lush and thriving forest.

He got the job done. How did he do it? By planting 30 million trees in less than 25 years.

It's hard to imagine one man planting that many trees—but Hakmet wasn't working alone. People liked his dream, so they helped. As these trees were planted, they took root and grew. Now, a forest stands where nothing used to grow.

You won't always see the wonderful things God's doing, but rest assured He's doing them! When you offer to help someone, it just makes the blessing bigger, better, and bolder. God's good idea can become a movement that changes history and the lives of people you love.

Planting trees can be satisfying, but this satisfaction gets bigger the longer the trees grow. They provide shade, invite birds, and let sunlight beautifully shimmer through their branches.

If you have a big project, work with other Christians to complete it. You'll be satisfied, and that satisfaction will continue for a long time. God may be asking you to do something really impressive. Just watch it grow! You serve a God who makes impossible things possible and hard things easy. He can straighten out crooked things. Nothing can stop God from doing what needs to be done. If He wants a forest to grow, He'll make it grow—even on the driest, dustiest hill. If He wants your friends or family members to know more about Him, He can use you to introduce Him to them.

Rely on God, accept help from His followers, and then watch big things happen!

I want to see You do big things, Father. You will do these things with or without me, but I want to do them with You. Help me spot opportunities to step up, step out, and step into Your plan.

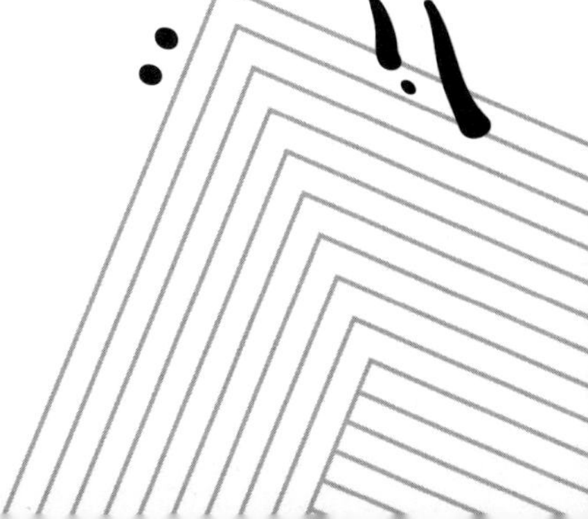

DAY 54

BEYOND SIGHT OF A GREAT VIEW

Faith is being sure we will get what we hope for. It is being sure of what we cannot see.

HEBREWS 11:1

No one likes to be pulled over by the police. It can make you think you're going to jail. It can make you feel embarrassed if someone you know drives by. It makes you nervous.

In Germany, however, hidden cameras take pictures of speeders, and the police send them tickets in the mail. One man received such a ticket. . .and was shocked to see a picture of his dog driving the car! At least that's what it looked like. What had actually happened was the dog had moved to the side of the real driver. So when the camera took the picture, it seemed a dog was driving the speeding car.

Police officers had to have faith that there was a person (not a dog) driving the car. They couldn't see the driver, but they needed to believe what they couldn't see.

People can see you do good things, but they may miss the fact that God's doing a greater work just out of their sight. They might think you're an impressive human being but miss the fact that you couldn't do any of this if God weren't inspiring you to do it. You yourself might even forget God's role in the good you do. You might want to take the credit. But when you do that, you're like that picture of a dog driving a car. It can't be true, but you're willing to let people think it might be. That means you could be accepting honor that really belongs to God.

Don't pretend to be the hero of God's story. Instead, be

happy that God's doing something great—and that you get to walk with Him when He does. You should then share that story with people who are curious about how such a good thing can happen.

Let them know who's *really* behind the wheel!

I love Your story, God. I'm glad that You want me to be part of it. I don't want to pretend that the good things You do are because of me. I'm just paying attention to where You go and then following along.

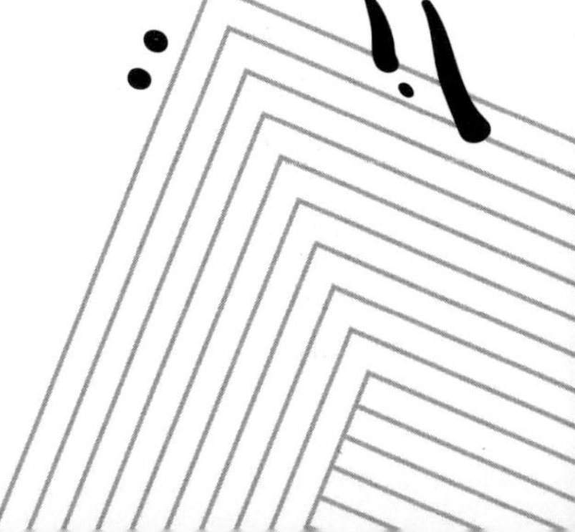

DAY 55

THE PLACE WHERE GOOD IDEAS BEGIN

Hold to the words of truth. . . . Teach the truth and show those who are against the truth that they are wrong.
Titus 1:9

A group of high school students in Virginia was asked to come up with a bill that a senator could introduce on the Senate floor. It happens every year, but this year was special—this time, the bill was debated, voted on, and passed into a law! This law allows people who live in Virginia to list their blood type on their driver's license. This is a big deal because if someone is in an accident, that person's driver's license can give healthcare workers enough information to perform a blood transfusion if needed. No one is forced to put the information on their license, but the new law means they can if they believe it would be helpful.

You get to introduce good ideas, and there's no better place to go for those ideas than the Bible. These are really great ideas because they are God's ideas—there's no limit to how much you can learn. It might be easier to pick a few Bible verses and believe you've learned everything, but that's not how it works. The more you read the Bible, the more you'll learn. Read it more than once. Read it every day if you can. What you learn helps you know what is true and what is false—and that's important!

God isn't finished with helping people come up with good ideas. He starts this journey with you by making sure you understand how important relationships are. He wants to be your friend, and He wants you to be a friend to others. He wants you to help people because you've learned how to love them. . .and you'll learn this only when you begin to understand how much Jesus loves you.

I need to learn how valuable Your Word is, Lord. I've learned a lot from Bible verses, but reading the Bible from start to finish will help me read all the parts of Your story that I've missed. Help me learn so that I can share some of Your really great ideas.

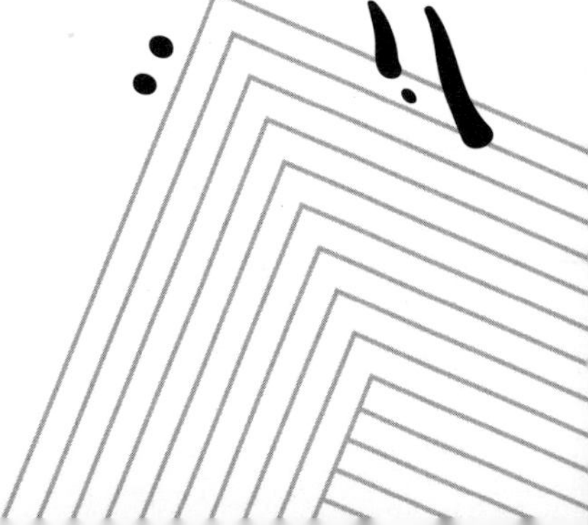

DAY 56

AIDEN'S UMBRELLA GIFT

Love does not give up. Love is kind. Love is not jealous. Love does not put itself up as being important. Love has no pride. Love does not do the wrong thing. Love never thinks of itself. Love does not get angry. Love does not remember the suffering that comes from being hurt by someone. . . . Love never comes to an end.

1 Corinthians 13:4–5, 8

The rain was falling in Illinois, so nine-year-old Aiden brought his umbrella to school. He was glad he did. He opened the school doors after the final bell and heard the slapping sound of raindrops on the sidewalks. Other students rushed by on their way to waiting cars and buses.

As he splashed along through the rain, he suddenly noticed something. Sitting in her wheelchair was the school librarian waiting for a public transit bus. Without hesitation, Aiden walked over, opened his umbrella, spread it over the librarian, and waited with her.

In that moment, a boy and an adult listened to raindrops making an impression on an umbrella. . .while the young boy's kindness made an impression on the librarian.

Whether Aiden realized it or not, his act of kindness was more than kindness—it's what the Bible calls love. This type of love is patient and puts others first.

You don't have to have an umbrella to show love to other people like Aiden did. You can care for your family, help your neighbors, and show thoughtfulness toward your friends in all sorts of ways.

Love isn't just something you feel—it's something you do. A love that only feels isn't God's idea of love at all. God's kind of love means going above and beyond to help people, even when they don't seem to deserve it. It's an investment that may never be returned. This might seem like an unfair trade, but it's actually a rare and wonderful gift. Unlike selfishness, love will be *remembered*.

For Aiden, his display of love was an umbrella in the rain. What will it look like for you?

I want to choose love as a gift to others, Father. Teach me more and help me learn.

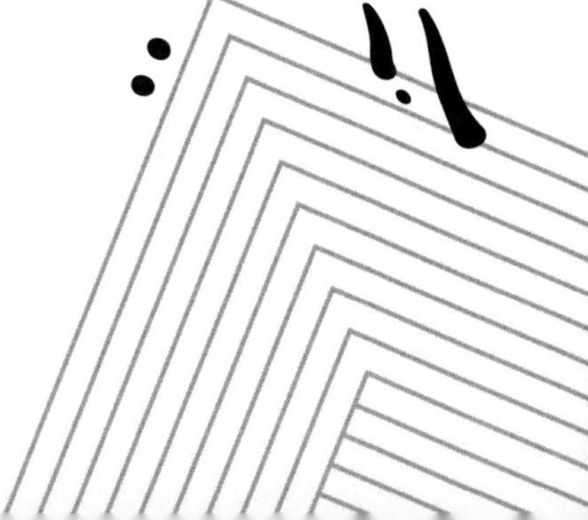

DAY 57

COMING HOME

Even before the world was made, God chose us for Himself because of His love. He planned that we should be holy and without blame as He sees us. God already planned to have us as His own children. This was done by Jesus Christ. In His plan God wanted this done.

Ephesians 1:4–5

Duke's life hasn't been easy, but he's made an impression on those who've met him. He is a mixed breed dog who was discovered in Kosovo by soldiers. The dog would come to see them every day. He was hungry, but he stayed to keep the soldiers company. This meant a lot to them because they were all far from home.

The soldiers looked forward to Duke's daily visits. They wanted to take the dog home with them, but sadly, the dog suddenly stopped coming. Eventually, the soldiers returned home.

New friends in Kosovo kept looking for Duke until they finally found him. He had suffered a bullet wound. The people of Kosovo took care of Duke, and after he recovered from his wounds, he was sent to soldiers in America. There, one of the soldiers from the beginning of the story adopted him.

When you discovered God, it was because He had something you needed more than anything else. If you didn't stay with Him, you eventually came back. That's because what He could give was something you couldn't find anywhere else. And when you decided it was worth it to stay with Him, He adopted you into His family. He made you a son. He prepared all the things you would need in the future. God took your wounds and healed you—and when the time is right, He will bring you home.

Duke had no idea that he would find his forever home on a military base in Kosovo. He was just looking for food. This dog was trying to meet his needs, but the new plan was much bigger than Duke could ever understand. Similarly, you might look for God for encouragement, but you'll end up with forgiveness and a forever life with Him.

Look for God—only He can offer the perfect plan!

Thank You, God, for helping me, adopting me, and then showing me more good than I could've ever imagined.

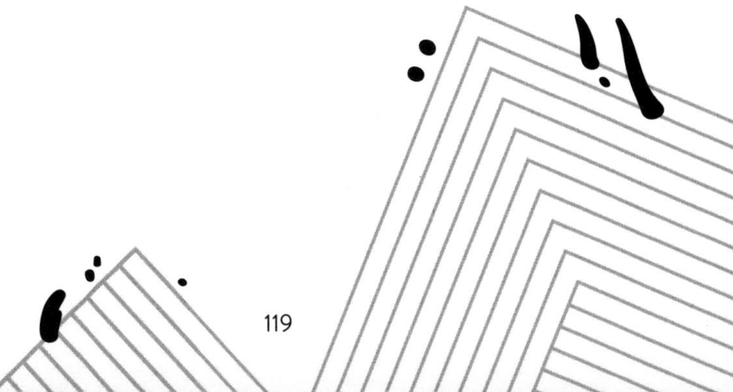

DAY 58

BLIND SPEED

God is my Helper. The Lord is the One
Who keeps my soul alive.
PSALM 54:4

Dan wasn't able to see, but he did something most people think a blind person shouldn't be able to do: he got behind the wheel of a car and drove fast—*really* fast. This courageous man reached a speed of 211 miles per hour. Before that, the fastest a blind person had ever driven was 200 miles per hour.

Dan had been blinded in a racing accident ten years before he set this record. He loves to race, and he never let his blindness stop him. His car, in fact, was custom made for blind drivers.

You may not have known that blind people could drive a car, but in some situations, they can. You may not be able to do everything, but in some situations, God can help you do what everyone thought was impossible.

God helps weak people do strong things. He makes impossible things a reality. He encourages big dreams that have a small possibility of success. He does this because without Him, nothing really meaningful would ever get done.

When you begin to think your plans are all up to you, get ready to watch them fail. Don't stop asking God for help or relying on Him to show up. Don't take credit for what happens. The more you leave God out of your plans, the less likely the plan is to succeed.

If you need help, if you just can't do things on your own,

then now's the perfect time to ask God to help. He can. He will. He wants to. And if God helps, then there's zero chance of failure. The only time failure happens is when you reject God's help or if He says no.

Dan drove a car blind, but he had the help of other people who made this act possible. You can do big things too whenever you have the help of a God who makes *all* things possible.

I'm weak, but You're strong, Lord. I can dream, but You can do all things. I can ask for help, and You can help me. Help me remember that I need You to be my partner in everything I do.

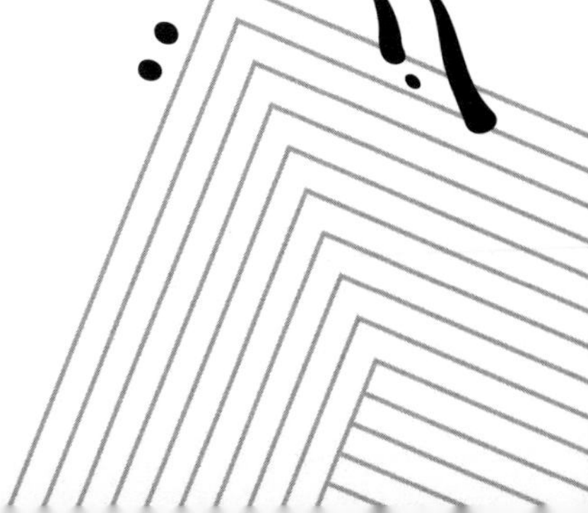

DAY 59

A RIDE OF RESPECT

"Show respect to the person with white hair. Honor an older person and you will honor your God."
LEVITICUS 19:32

Independence is important to people as they get older. When people retire, they might worry about not being able to enjoy going where they want to go and seeing things they want to see. That's why some people in Scotland created a bike with a two-seat bench in the front. Someone else rides and steers the bike while older riders sit safely in front and watch the world go by.

People who've watched them say these older adults are all smiles as they feel the exciting freedom of riding a bike with no fear of falling. These safe bike rides, some say, have given them freedom they thought they had lost and might never get back. There are now thousands of these special bikes in use around the world helping to bring freedom to those who may no longer be able to ride a bike on their own.

God wants you to remember that older people often have a lot of wisdom. They have lived more life than you have. They know that some things work (like following God) while other things don't (like trying to do everything on your own). If you listen, these older men and women may be able to help you. Making fun of them never shows respect—God wants you to help them whenever you can.

There is another reason to respect people who are older than you. If you won't honor whomever God said you should honor, then how could you possibly honor God? Obedience, after all, is a great way to show that you're willing to follow God. It's hard to show that God means something to you when you decide you won't do what He asks you to do!

I may not know everything, but You do, Father. Because You're wise, You tell me to respect people who are older than I am. Give me the wisdom to make that choice. That choice will always be easier when I honor and respect You first.

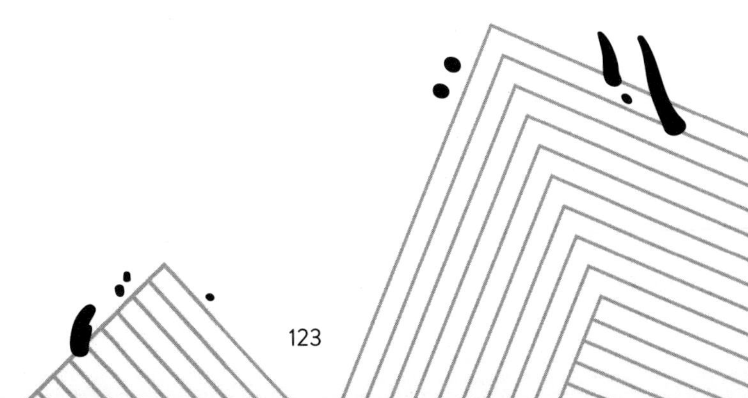

DAY 60

FEAST WISELY

Keep yourself growing in God-like living. Growing strong in body is all right but growing in God-like living is more important. It will not only help you in this life now but in the next life also.

1 Timothy 4:7–8

You probably think that all bees sting, but not in Peru. This country has a very large population of "stingless" bees. Like regular honeybees, they make honey. But because this honey is made from the pollen of many unique plants, it can be used as medicine! This is probably why Peruvian honey farmers make a lot more money than beekeepers anywhere else.

Scientists work with these beekeepers to identify all the honey's benefits. When the bees take pollen from one type of plant to another, it can change what benefits the honey has. So far, this honey has been used to treat colds, upper-respiratory-tract infections, diabetes, stomach problems, arthritis, and cancer—and it all depends on what the bee eats.

Clearly, these bees can do some pretty amazing things! However, if they got their pollen from different plants, then their honey wouldn't have the same effect. Suddenly, the story wouldn't be quite as interesting.

The Christian's life should look something like these stingless bees. You can make the biggest impression on people when you live a God-like life. When you feast on God's teaching found in His Word, the life you live can be used to treat the illness that many people feel without God. He can use what you're learning to help you help others. But if you don't enjoy His feast, then you'll never be able to help others discover healing.

To make this simple, let's just say that you can't help people know about God if you don't know Him very well yourself. If you won't learn, then how could what you share be helpful? Just like Peruvian bees, the good you can share depends on who you spend time with.

I always have a choice, God. I can spend time with You or spend it doing anything else. When You're my second choice, I'll miss chances to tell other people about You. My life won't be as helpful, and that makes You sad. Be my first choice—always.

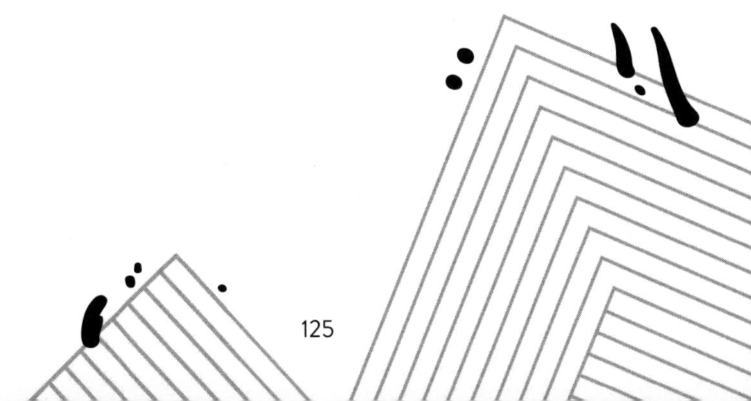

DAY 61

CLAIMING GOOD NEWS

"For the Lord says, 'When seventy years are completed for Babylon, I will visit you and keep My promise to you. I will bring you back to this place. For I know the plans I have for you,' says the Lord, 'plans for well-being and not for trouble, to give you a future and a hope. Then you will call upon Me and come and pray to Me, and I will listen to you. You will look for Me and find Me, when you look for Me with all your heart.' "

JEREMIAH 29:10–13

Sometimes, people throw things away because they are tired of them; other times, it's because they have no idea what they are. In 2017, Jared came across some "trash" that had been cleared out of an old barn. But even though its owner saw no use for it, Jared saw otherwise.

That trash was worth hundreds of thousands of dollars. Each piece was wrapped in plastic. But underneath the plastic was artwork from a once-well-respected artist. Jared, a mechanic, was once the caretaker of a rare set of art pieces. The artist passed away years ago and was almost forgotten. But suddenly, this "trash" brought fresh contributions to the art world again.

God never said you had to be a preacher to share His impressive collection of good news. God's good news is available to all, and all are allowed to share it. This news should never be forgotten—it is a priceless treasure. Unexpectedly discovering this treasure can be awe-inspiring.

Some people, however, don't think this news is worth much, so they walk away, leaving it sitting until someone else finds it. But the good news about God's good news is that anyone who wants it can find it. No one needs to be left out.

A lot of things changed for Jared when he claimed someone's trash and discovered a treasure. Even more can change for you when you claim God's treasure. Neither your present nor your future will ever be the same.

Don't leave God's treasure behind.

Lord, I've found the most important treasure of all—You. You don't hide, and You're ready to be found by anyone. I need to point to Your treasure so that other people know it exists. I can't make anyone take Your treasure, but maybe You can help them see what amazing things this treasure has done for me.

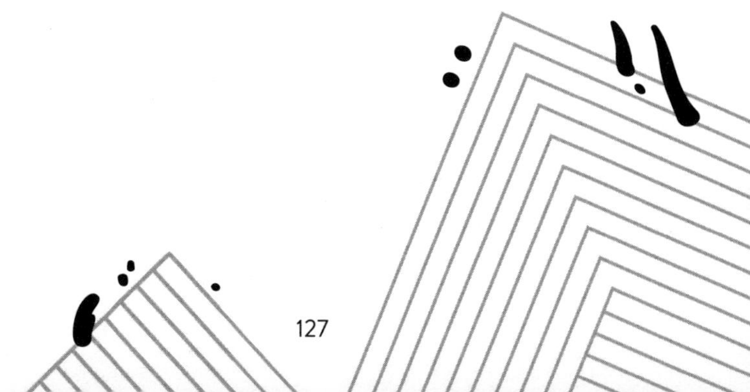

DAY 62

ORANGE VESTS

I pray that the great God and Father of our Lord Jesus Christ may give you the wisdom of His Spirit. Then you will be able to understand the secrets about Him as you know Him better. I pray that your hearts will be able to understand. I pray that you will know about the hope given by God's call. I pray that you will see how great the things are that He has promised to those who belong to Him.

EPHESIANS 1:17–18

You've probably seen men and women in orange safety vests working beside the road. This outfit helps travelers notice them—and realize they need to slow down. What you may not know, however, is that the people who design these vests may themselves never be able to notice them. How is that possible? These vests are often created by people who have trouble seeing. Some of them are totally blind. These workers create safety clothing for the military and first responders. Each year, they sell more than five million dollars' worth of their products.

The Bible tells the story of a man who had always been blind. But when this man met Jesus, he experienced a miracle—he could see for the first time ever! In response, some people complained, some argued, and others blamed. But all this man could say was this: "One thing I know. I was blind, but now I can see" (John 9:25). He wanted other people to make up their own minds about Jesus' miracle.

Not everyone who was born blind will see again. But that doesn't mean these people can't do amazing things! Helen Keller, for example, couldn't see *or hear*, but she still learned how to understand and communicate with others. Other blind people have invented things like cruise control, submarines, and text to speech. . .and one blind woman even wrote more than 8,000 Christian songs!

Sometimes, God heals; other times, He uses hard things to teach new lessons that couldn't be learned any other way. People who overcome limitations are often remembered and celebrated for their accomplishments.

When I struggle, Father, help me remember I'm not the only one and that You love me no matter what.

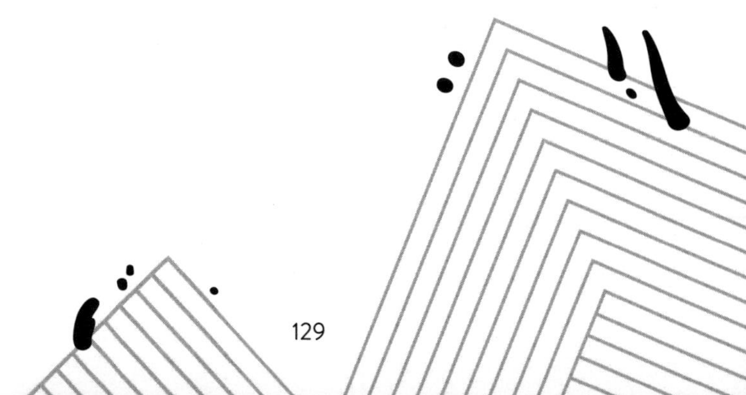

DAY 63

THE BIGGEST—THE BEST

"O Lord God! See, You have made the heavens and the earth by Your great power and by Your long arm! Nothing is too hard for You!"
JEREMIAH 32:17

If you've ever been to a rodeo, then you know cowboys wear big belt buckles. Some have joked that you could even take those belt buckles and use them as plates if you really needed to.

One company that makes belt buckles decided it was time to go big or go home. They created a buckle that was nearly 15 feet across—a new world record for the biggest belt buckle. The buckle was sent in four parts to its permanent home in Texas, where everything was put together.

If you want to know who holds the record for the most power, that would be God. The most love? God. The most forgiveness? God. The most faithful? If you guessed God, you're right!

People try to break records every day, but they're challenging other people—not God. It's important to remember that you'll always need God's help, no matter how many good things you do. If you've broken His rules even once, then you can never be perfect without Him. He can take His perfection and apply it to your sin and say you're not guilty. You can never do that on your own.

God is bigger, wiser, and more caring than anyone who's ever lived. He is completely different than you. It's never wise to compare your best effort with His perfection. He can't be beaten. That's why it's so incredible that this God loves you. He doesn't need a book of world records—no one can successfully challenge God.

Discover joy in knowing that the record holder for all good things wants to be your friend and spend time with you! But here's the big question: Do you want to spend time with Him?

Spending time with You is amazing, God. You can do what I can't, and yet You love to spend time with me. You're perfect, unlike me, yet You want to forgive me. You're generous even when I'm selfish, yet You keep giving good gifts.

DAY 64

THE THINGS YOU DO

If I can give thanks to God for my food, why should anyone say that I am wrong about eating food I can give thanks for? So if you eat or drink or whatever you do, do everything to honor God.

1 Corinthians 10:30–31

Jonathan is very smart, and he wants to do big things. After finishing high school, he sent applications to nearly 30 colleges. . .and nearly every school accepted him! He received four million dollars in scholarships. There wasn't a single school that didn't want Jonathan to come.

Jonathan is a very skilled writer and inventor. He's seeking a career that will help him continue improving people's lives through his inventions. People are paying attention to Jonathan.

You might not be an inventor, you might not like to play sports, and you may not even enjoy video games. But whatever it is that you like to do, honor God with it.

Yesterday, you learned there's no one bigger or better than God. He can help you do the right thing, and the more you obey God, the more things He will ask you to do. These are big, important things you could never do on your own.

God doesn't make you do what you don't want to do. He just works on your heart until you agree that what He asks you to do is right. He says that the love you have for Him will show up when you choose to obey. Why? It's not very loving to say you want to follow God and then decide He's not worth the effort.

Whatever good things you can do, do them as well as possible—after all, you're doing them to honor God. Don't do these things to get noticed—doing so will honor you, not God. Only one can be honored. If you're honored, then God is not honored.

Every choice you make will either honor God. . .or it won't. The Bible can teach you how to tell the difference so that you can choose to do things that honor God.

I don't care if anyone else recognizes me for doing good things, Lord. I just want to honor You and hear You say, "Well done."

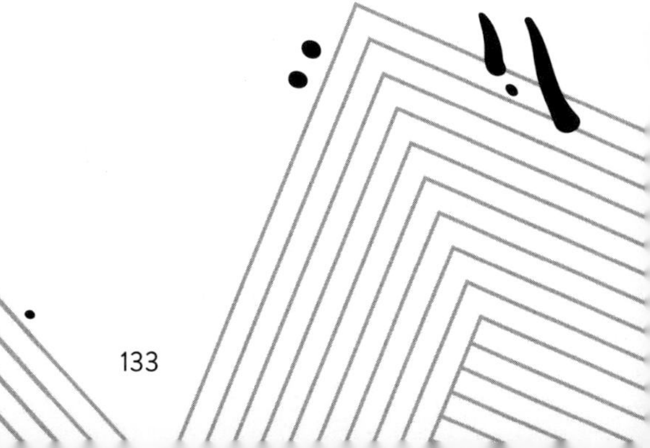

DAY 65

BE THE HAMBURGER FISH

You are a chosen group of people. . . . You are a holy nation. You belong to God. He has done this for you so you can tell others how God has called you out of darkness into His great light.

1 Peter 2:9

When most people go fishing, they expect a fish on the end of their line—they don't want boots and sticks. They also want the fish to *look* like a fish. But some creatures that lurk in the waters aren't so easily recognized. A fisherman in the waters off Norway once caught some impressive (but unusual!) creatures that looked nothing like fish. One reminded some people of a baby dragon. Another looked like a hamburger, complete with a bun. Still another resembled a jam-filled doughnut.

People are interested in the unusual. They want to see pictures of strange fish and unusual animals, plants, and insects. They catch our attention because they're so different from other things we know.

When you follow Jesus, you might seem like a hamburger fish, jam fish, or baby dragon. People see you as unusual, so they want to know more. They'll spend time trying to spot the differences between your life and theirs.

It's not surprising that if Jesus makes you a new creation, other people will notice. And when they do, they'll be curious. And when they're curious, they'll want to know more. Maybe that's why God wants you to be different. Acting like everyone else will never cause people to ask questions. If you blend into the crowd, you're just not as interesting.

When you are God's kind of different, you represent Him well. But if you are different just to gain attention, you may not be representing God at all.

Chosen, set apart, and belonging to God—all are reasons for you to be different. It's this difference that can make a difference in someone else.

Sometimes, Father, I worry about what people might think if I started looking more like You and less like them. But if that means even more people get to know You, then help me learn to be comfortable with being Your kind of different.

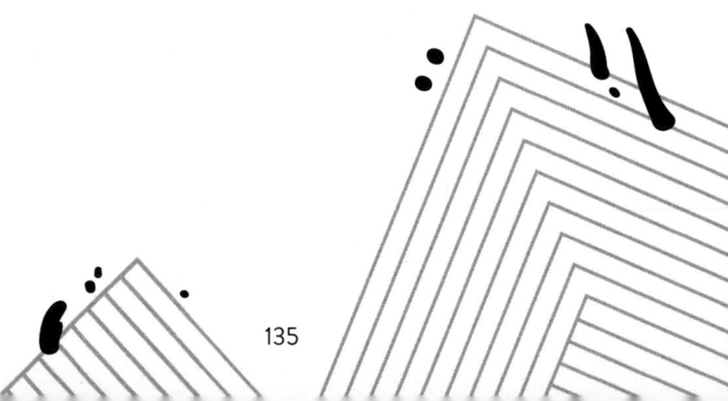

DAY 66

YOUR NEW HOME

"God will take away all their tears. There will be no more death or sorrow or crying or pain. All the old things have passed away."

REVELATION 21:4

If you had the chance to do something important, would you do it?

A teacher in Virginia had one of those big and important ideas. What if she had her students visit pets at the local animal shelter and spend time with over 20 animals that struggled to find forever homes? Those students discovered the animals' personalities and then wrote letters to people who might adopt the animals. When people came to the shelter to adopt a pet, they found a wall of letters from these students on display. That way, the visitors could read all about the pets before they ever met them.

This big idea worked. One by one, the letters were removed from the shelter as the animals were taken to their forever homes.

God did something a little different for you. He offered to adopt you no matter what others thought of you. Then He wrote a letter (the Bible) to help train you as a newly adopted son—and to help others understand what you're learning. God takes misfits and makes them masterpieces. He takes outcasts and makes them outstanding. He takes "left-behinds" and loves them. His big idea works.

His home for you is amazing. One day, you'll be with Him,

and anything that has ever hurt you will vanish forever. Anything that made a tear leak from your eye won't bother you. All the things that you needed to forgive will no longer exist. All things will be new in God's heaven, and sadness won't be welcome.

But before that happens, God has big and important things for you to do. Ask Him to help you learn what those are, and then do your best for the God that made you a son. Tell Him you're grateful that you weren't left in a shelter without hope.

God has your forever home waiting. . .and someday, He'll show up to give you a tour.

A future without pain sounds really good, God.
I can't wait to meet You face to face.

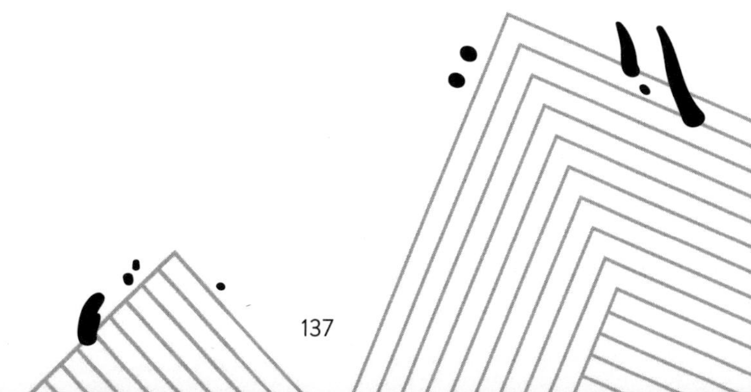

DAY 67

IMPOSSIBLE OUTCOMES MEET GOD

[Jesus said,] "In the world you will have much trouble. But take hope! I have power over the world!"

JOHN 16:33

Cory had a bad day, one that could've changed his attitude about life. He broke several ribs, both arms, and his spine in a bicycle accident. Doctors told Cory he would never walk again.

But Cory didn't like that idea. He wanted to do his best to learn how to walk once his bones healed. He was paralyzed, but Cory wanted something different than a wheelchair.

After countless surgeries and many painful, tiring hours in physical therapy, Cory started taking steps. The steps were hard, and he walked blocks instead of miles. But even though he relied on crutches and leg braces, this man's hard work had paid off—he could walk again.

Bad things happen to everyone. Jesus never said that Christians would be able to skip trouble. But Jesus' power is greater than anything on earth, His love is deeper than the deepest well, and His forgiveness is impossibly generous.

He's compassionate with Christians who live through trouble. He's close to those who feel like they've been crushed, broken, and left behind. He makes weak people strong, and He cares deeply about you. It's always worthwhile to talk to God about your struggles, seek His help, and ask for an impossible outcome.

King David faced a giant. . .and won. Daniel faced lions . . .and God shut their mouths. If something has never been done, that might just mean no one has ever asked God to do it before. The Bible is full of examples.

God doesn't have to say yes to every prayer you pray, but your prayer shows Him that you believe He could—as long as it's the best solution for your need.

When the impossible meets God, the impossible changes its mind.

Some days are really hard, Lord. It's good to know that this doesn't surprise You. Help me when I work through hard times. Trying to do this alone is impossible. Only You can change my outcome. Help me to accept Your answer and to thank You for the help You give me.

DAY 68

THE VALUE OF DOING

Happy are all who honor the Lord with fear, and who walk in His ways. For you will eat the fruit of your hands. You will be happy and it will be well with you.

Psalm 128:1–2

Do you have a hobby? What do you enjoy doing in your spare time? Good and wholesome activities are important for people of any age—including you. When you use your mind and the skills you've learned, you may meet people with similar interests and start feeling better about life. Maybe that's why people love to play sports, sing, or make cool things.

People have known this was true for a very long time—now, science finally agrees. But even before anyone realized it, God said it was good for people to work hard and be satisfied in what they do.

When you read the Bible, you'll discover all kinds of good things God wants you to do. That'll keep you busy with things that leave you feeling better about life. While you're doing these things with God's help, you'll never be alone.

Hobbies can help a boy like you find satisfaction in learning to do something well. Sometimes, hobbies even turn into careers. God gave you a life and a purpose, so finding satisfaction in what you do is important. When there's nothing to do, there's not much to learn or share. Doing nothing won't accomplish anything—it just leads to selfishness. God thinks that's a bad idea. Why? Selfishness is the easiest way to begin feeling lonely and bored, and it can leave you feeling like nothing really matters.

God has a plan, and this plan usually involves doing something. God asks you to love other people—and love *always* does something. It helps when help is needed, and it shows up when someone hurts.

What will you do today?

I don't want to be bored, Father. It makes me feel like I missed out on something good. Give me good things to try, and help me learn skills to do these things well. Help me use these skills to love and help others. I want to be satisfied in doing whatever You want me to do.

DAY 69

PRICELESS AND NOT FOR SALE

"I give them life that lasts forever. They will never be punished. No one is able to take them out of My hand. My Father Who gave them to Me is greater than all. No one is able to take them out of My Father's hand."

John 10:28–29

Sometimes, the most unusual things are found in an auction house. Charles, the owner of an auction house in England, discovered this truth when he bought an old vase to sell. It was unique, for sure, but not worth much. Or so he thought.

Before auction day, he had the vase examined by some experts. Charles was glad he made that decision. The vase was actually 400 years old—and it was sold for a whopping 20,000 dollars!

It's possible that your family has treasure hiding away in the attic, basement, or storage locker. You might even want to start a family treasure hunt. Whether you find anything or not, such a hunt will teach you a lot about your family's past. And as you look through old things, make sure to ask them lots of questions. You might be surprised at the treasure you find!

God calls you a treasure, and He has no intention of putting you up at auction. You're priceless, and God never wants to lose any of His masterpieces. Nothing could ever convince Him you're not worth the effort of making into a new creation.

God doesn't keep looking for bigger and better things. He pours effort into *you*, and He reaches out to those who need to know Him. He increases your value by working on your life and encouraging every good choice you make.

You're worth more than you think—way more than any amount of money you could ever earn. The love God has for you has never changed at any moment in your life—even when you might have tried to run away from Him.

Sometimes, You put more effort into me than I put into serving You, God. You have always loved me, even when I doubted You or didn't want anything to do with You. May I always remember I'm loved. . .and then love You in return.

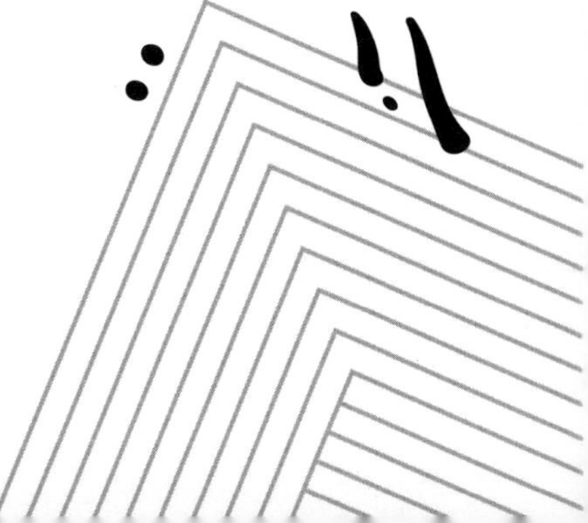

DAY 70

BE READY TO LISTEN

Do not always be thinking about your own plans only. Be happy to know what other people are doing.

PHILIPPIANS 2:4

Sometimes, people need a little help. And sometimes, people see the need and step up to help.

Burhan is 72 years old, and when cancer struck, he didn't have the energy to keep up his yard or his home's outer appearance. Soon, people started noticing his yard for all the wrong reasons.

That's when 60 volunteers stepped up to cut, trim, and clean his yard. In one day, they managed to get everything back in shape. This made Burhan relieved, and the neighbors were happy for him too.

People have good days, but they also have struggles. They need someone to listen, and that person could be you. You shouldn't do this just so other people will know all the good things you do—no, you've got to be *interested* in learning more about other people.

It's never wrong to think about what you're doing, but it's also never wrong to pay attention to what others are doing. Share the good things that happen in your life, but also listen to other people who haven't been so lucky. You might be able to help. How? Well, you're certainly able to pray for them! People are encouraged when someone like you is compassionate enough to listen. So start there—after all, most people won't even do that.

What if you took an interest in knowing more about someone's hobby? What if you asked an older man what life was like when he was your age? What if you asked people about the best part of their day. . .and really listened? This might just bring you closer to others. They might believe no one cares. But when you do this for them, it shows you think they're important and what they have to say is worthwhile.

Love. Listen. Help.

I would be honored if people thought of me as someone who listened to them, Lord. Help me hear and remember the concerns of others. Help invite people to speak—and then let my own words be few.

DAY 71

COMPARISON SHOPPING

Everyone should look at himself and see how he does his own work. Then he can be happy in what he has done. He should not compare himself with his neighbor.
GALATIANS 6:4

You might be tall (or maybe you want to be), but very few people are as tall as the Trapp family. This Minnesota family has an average height of just over six feet, eight inches. They're in the record books as the tallest family.

The tallest member of the Trapp family is seven feet, three inches tall. One of the brothers was taller than his teachers. . .when he was in first grade! The family says the worst thing about being that tall is having to duck when walking through doorways.

It can be easy to compare yourself to others. Perhaps you feel badly because someone does something better, or maybe you're just happy you're not as bad at something as someone else is. It depends on whom you decide to compare yourself to. You'll almost always be better or worse than *somebody*, and it will make you feel something God doesn't want you to feel. You'll either want to be better than a person or you'll want everyone to know how good you are.

You could compare yourself to the Trapps and wonder why you can't be as tall. You may compare yourself to a sports figure and think, *Why do I even practice? I'll never be that good.* Or you might make yourself feel better by looking at people who are worse than you at something. But that'd be at the expense of someone else. If you're supposed to love people and pay attention to what they are interested in, then this kind of thinking is off limits.

Stop looking for anyone you can compare yourself to. Instead, compare yourself to Jesus and learn that He can help you do better.

There's nothing hard about comparing myself to others, Father. It feels nice to think that I'm better than someone else. Because I'm not perfect, let me compare myself to You instead. Then let me thank You for loving me enough to forgive my failure.

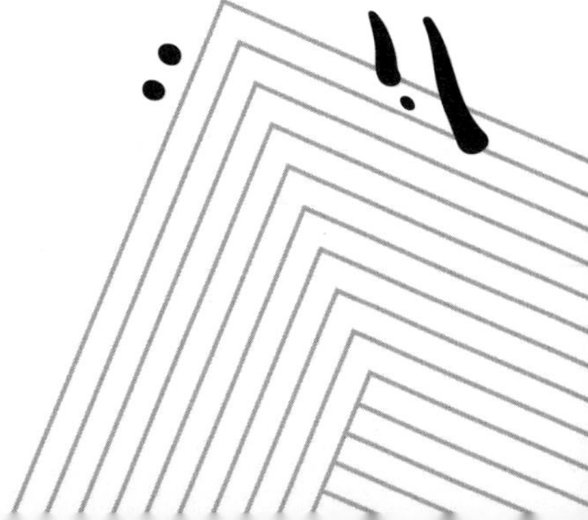

DAY 72

ONE REALLY SMALL BOOK

Your Word have I hid in my heart,
that I may not sin against You.
Psalm 119:11

There's a book that's so small you could put it in a very small bubble and wear it like the gem on a necklace. If you sneezed while holding it, you might lose it. This book is less than a quarter inch tall and a quarter inch wide. When it was sold at auction, someone was willing to pay nearly 5,000 dollars for it. This book was created as a fundraising project in 1952 to help pay for efforts to rebuild after World War II.

So what is this small book, anyway? It's a Bible.

You'd need to use a magnifying lens to read it, but it's all there. Hopefully, the new owners don't lose this very small book.

The Bible comes in all sizes, and you can even read it online. It's God's thoughts, so it should be important to you. And if you memorize some of what you read, then even if you can't find your Bible right away, you can remember some of what God thinks about the problems you're facing.

God's book is more than a trinket to store in your room—it's a letter from God Himself! How can you know what God wants if you don't read His instructions? Why would you guess what God wants when you can know for sure?

If you need a Bible, you should ask for one. Maybe your family or the church you go to will get one for you. And once you start reading the Bible, you'll find answers to all your important questions. It may not help you pass your math or chemistry test, but it does contain history, advice, instructions, and important information about what God wants you to do. Get to know God better by reading His instructions.

You never want me to have to guess what You want me to do, God. The words in Your book help me know You better, follow You with confidence, and see what I need to do to stay close to You. I want that, and I'm grateful You made sure I have it.

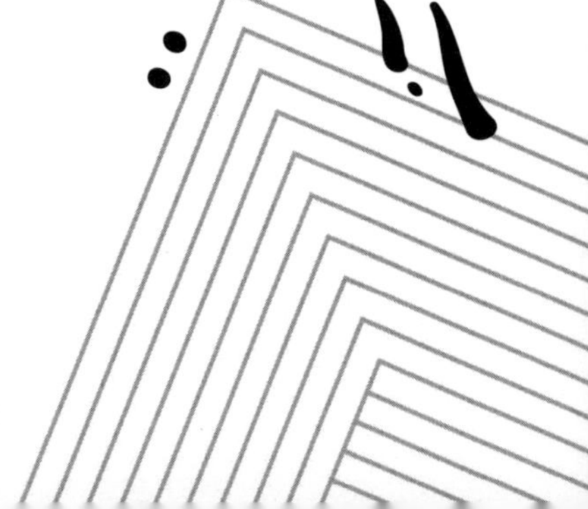

DAY 73

NOT YOUR TYPICAL HOUSE CATS

Put on the things God gives you to fight with. Then you will not fall into the traps of the devil. Our fight is not with people. It is against the leaders and the powers and the spirits of darkness in this world. It is against the demon world that works in the heavens.

Ephesians 6:11–12

Many people who find a lost cat or dog take care of it until they can find the owner. That's what Kyran, who lived in India, tried to do. One day, he stumbled across some kittens who were very cold. He had compassion on them and, after failing to find their mama, took them home.

That was a mistake. Once the kittens warmed up from the cold weather after a few days, they stopped meowing. . .and started growling. You see, these weren't ordinary kittens—they were leopards!

Kyran figured there might be a better place for them than in his house.

Most people would make the same choice. Leopards don't make good houseguests. They are wild animals that like to hunt. Having a full-grown leopard in your home just isn't a good idea.

God has given all the instructions you need to avoid things that can hurt you. God's enemy, Satan, wants to spend time with you, but not in a good way. He's like a leopard who disguises himself as a harmless kitten. You start out thinking it's a good idea to hang out with him, but soon this kitten is growling and trying to destroy you.

God can help you recognize things that can harm your journey with Him. He wants you to avoid those things, but if they follow you, He gives you details on how to stand strong against them.

Love doesn't destroy. People who love you want the best for you. And if you love someone, you want the best for that person too. Truly, this world could use a lot more love. God started the trend of loving people, and you can keep it going.

Refuse to be a leopard.

I can sometimes be like a leopard, Lord. I bite, snarl, and growl while I say I love You. Help me want the best for others. Help me support other people and fight against anything that can destroy time with You.

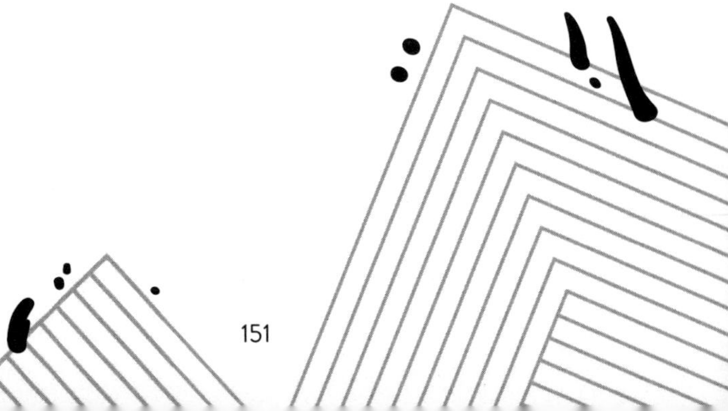

DAY 74

THE UNWISE ATTACK

[Jesus said,] "Love those who work against you. Do good to those who hate you."
LUKE 6:27

Arlene loves her home in the Rocky Mountains. She's used to seeing deer, yet they always impress her. At Christmastime, her family sits out an old 3-D archery target that has been transformed into a deer-shaped lawn decoration. The problem? Real deer, thinking the fake deer is a rival, soon start attacking it! Every year, Arlene's family sets up the Christmas deer—and every year, at least one buck deer tries to destroy it. The unusual lawn decoration has been broken many times. Arlene's family even installed lights on it to convince the deer that it's not a threat, yet it *still* gets attacked.

You might find yourself acting like a real deer attacking a fake one. Maybe you can't seem to recognize that what makes you angry isn't what you're really angry about. You might get mad at your mom, but really you're just mad at what she asked you to do—or maybe you're just mad at someone at school and decide to take it out on someone else.

It's not very wise to use your words to attack other people. God says you should choose to love people, even those who hate you. That can be very hard to do, but it's what God does every day—including for you. You didn't love God first—He loved you before you were born! He loved you first so that you would know what love looks like. And once you know that, it's a little easier to do the same thing for someone else.

People get hurt when anger shows up. People stop trusting when hate is around. But those same people are surprised when you choose to love instead. With love, there's always less hurt and more trust.

It's never a wise idea to lash out at other people, Father. It seems easier to hate and hurt others than it does to love and help them. But people need to know that hate is a very bad choice. Teach me how to do what You've always done for me.

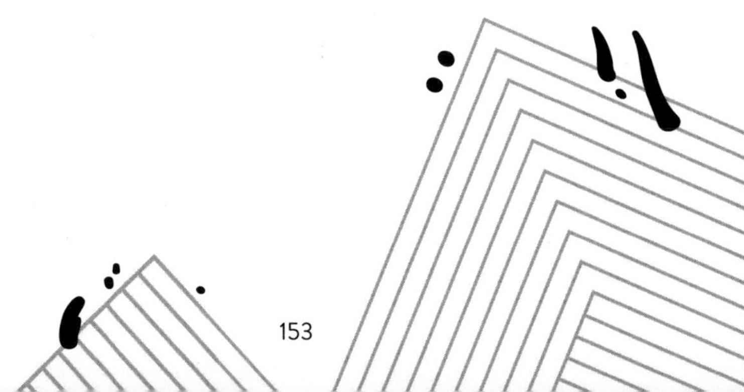

DAY 75

WHAT YOU ALREADY HAVE

"Your heart will be wherever your riches are."

LUKE 12:34

Every day, people donate items to thrift stores without realizing how valuable some of these items are. That includes things like envelopes of cash or gold rings.

Some things you don't even want to get rid of. In Denver, Colorado, a family brought a recliner to a second-hand store. They unloaded the recliner and went home. What they didn't know was that the family cat had crawled inside and was left behind! Don't worry, though—it was reunited with its family.

Usually, you want the things you value most to stay close. That could be something a grandparent gave you or something you worked hard to earn. It probably involves your family or friends. It should include God. Your greatest treasure will always be found in relationships. Your family is always worth more than money. Your friends can't be traded for cash. Your relationship with God is priceless.

Don't hide relationships in places where it's easy to forget them. Never be ashamed of a friendship with God. If He has your heart, then what you can earn is less important than what you already have.

If God is priceless, then do everything you can to stay connected to Him—He's the best friend you'll ever have. The Bible is filled with stories of men who valued their friendship with God so much that they were willing to suffer for it. This included men like Noah, Moses, Abraham, Hezekiah, David,

Solomon, John, Peter, Paul, and Barnabas. If you want to read some good stories, then spend some time in the Bible reading about men who loved God.

Will people remember your life's story for how much you valued relationships? People are forgetful, but they'll never forget how they feel about you.

God wants you to be memorable.

You're worth more than anything I'll ever own, God. I don't want to treat You like You're as common as fast food or a video game. You're so much more than that, even though I sometimes don't act like it. Help me stay focused on what's most valuable and important—You.

DAY 76

BE THE NEIGHBOR

The man said, "You must love the Lord your God with all your heart. You must love Him with all your soul. You must love Him with all your strength. You must love Him with all your mind. You must love your neighbor as you love yourself."

Luke 10:27

One buzzard in England was on the trip of a lifetime—but not in a way anyone expected. This big bird was just minding its own business in the middle of the road when suddenly it found itself stuck inside the front grill of a passing car. The driver didn't know anything had happened—she thought the small thump had been a rock.

The bird, thankfully unhurt, watched as the world whizzed by faster than it had ever flown. It had to be exciting. . .and probably a little frightening! In the end, the bird was released to fly again—just a bit slower than its unexpected car ride.

God wants to take you on an unexpected journey, the adventure of a lifetime! It can seem uncomfortable because it's unfamiliar, but He'll take care of you and make sure you have everything you need. With God, you'll be going places and doing things that are important and bring you joy.

Jesus talked to a man who seemed interested in going on this kind of journey. After Jesus asked him what God's Law said, the man answered with today's verse: to love God with all your heart, soul, strength, and mind, and then love your neighbor. His answer was full of wisdom and truth. Jesus then told the man that he should think of *everyone* he met as his neighbor.

That last part can be hard. Sometimes, you'll meet people you don't like and don't want to help. But Jesus said if you really love Him, then you will love other people too.

This will be the adventure you didn't know you needed!

Help me love You first with all that I am, Lord. Then help me love others because You love me. Let me see that when I obey Your command to love, it pleases You, helps others, and changes me.

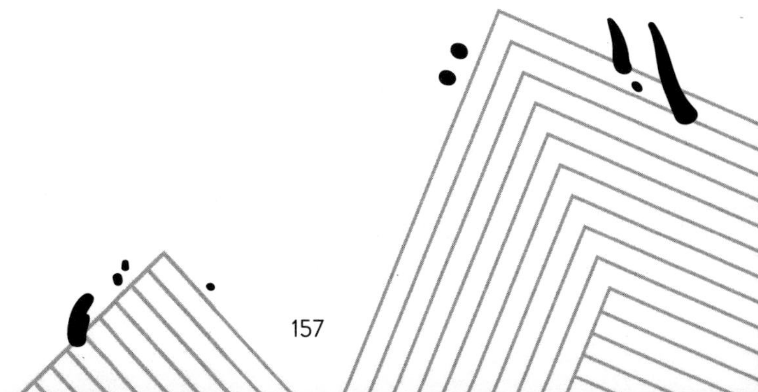

DAY 77

THE PROMISES YOU MAKE

This is what I think. You had better finish what you started a year ago. You were the first to want to give a gift of money. Now do it with the same strong desires you had when you started.

2 Corinthians 8:10–11

Zara was a teenager when she made a special choice—she learned how to fly a small airplane. She had the dream of being the youngest woman to fly all by herself around the world. It was a big dream, and the bad weather made things even harder. At times, Zara had to land her plane and wait for big storms to pass.

But eventually, this young lady completed her flight and landed back home in Belgium. It was one of the hardest things she'd ever encountered, but Zara finished what she started.

Second Corinthians 8:11 is part of a letter that apostle Paul wrote to the church in Corinth. The members of this church had promised to use some of their money to help, but it seemed like they might not follow through. Paul encouraged them to remember their original plan and finish what they started. He wanted them to keep their promise.

God wants you to keep the good promises you make. After all, *He* always does. God will continue keeping His promises, so He doesn't like it when you promise to do something and then change your mind. In fact, it seems He would rather you not make a promise than to break it!

Unkept promises can make people wonder if you really

can be trusted. And if you can't be trusted, then they might wonder if God is as faithful as you say He is.

God wants boys like you to be responsible and dependable. He wants other people to see that Christians are the most helpful people around. That doesn't always happen, but it's not because God changed His plans—it's usually because people think promises are meant to be broken. They aren't.

I need to remember that You don't break promises, Father. Sometimes, I intend to keep promises, but then they seem so hard that I forget ever making them. . .or I hope no one remembers. Help me take promise keeping as seriously as You do.

DAY 78
THE MESS

If we say that we have no sin, we lie to ourselves and the truth is not in us. . . . If we say we have not sinned, we make God a liar. And His Word is not in our hearts.

1 John 1:8, 10

When people think of their favorite birds, they might pick an eagle, a parrot, or maybe even a hummingbird. They don't usually think of crows. The sound a crow makes isn't exactly pleasant—many people even think crows are a nuisance.

In Sunnyvale, California, the crows have become a huge problem. They all happily gather downtown, making such a noise (and mess) that people want to stay away. The city tried all kinds of things to make the birds go away, but nothing seemed to work. . .until they stumbled across lasers.

Don't worry, these lasers can't hurt the crows, but the crows still don't like them. They get nervous around the little beams of light. So after the lasers were installed, the problem was fixed. Now, city employees don't need to clean the sidewalks nearly as much.

When you say you don't sin, it's like the people of Sunnyvale saying they've never seen a crow downtown. Sin exists everywhere, it makes a horrible noise, and it needs to be cleaned up. That's what God does, but He first needs you to admit that you've sinned and then tell Him all about it so that He can forgive you. He does the cleanup, but you first have to recognize the mess sin has made.

Sin is an unpleasant companion and a horrible friend. It

says you should do what you want, but what you want can hurt others. It can hurt you too.

You don't want to call God a liar, and you shouldn't lie to yourself. When God's Word finds a place deep in your heart, it will be easier to notice the mess sin has made. Only then can you request a cleaning.

I don't want to break Your rules, God, but I break them anyway. I just can't seem to help myself. It makes me sad, and I want to stop. Would You help me? Would You give me the strength to say no? Would You make me clean once more? Thank You.

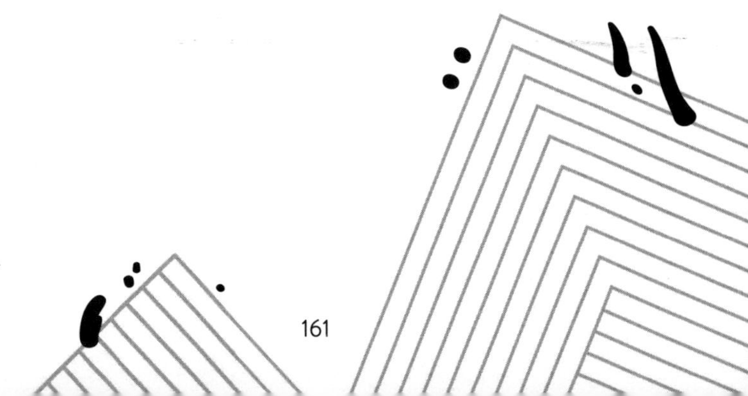

DAY 79

LIFE CHOICES

Listen! You who say, "Today or tomorrow we will go to this city and stay a year and make money." You do not know about tomorrow. What is your life? It is like fog. You see it and soon it is gone.

James 4:13–14

Broccoli may not be your favorite vegetable, but for Chloe one day, it wasn't just nasty—it was terrifying! You see, Chloe lives in Australia, and when she picked up some broccoli for an evening meal, she had no idea she would be hosting an uninvited guest. Lurking deep within the broccoli stalks was a crawling, angry scorpion.

Her father-in-law was visiting, and he took care of the scorpion. It's not clear whether Chloe and guests ate any of the broccoli. The grocery store manager did say this didn't happen very often. (That's nice to know!)

You can treat life like nothing unusual will ever happen, but sometimes you'll come face to face with things as strange as a scorpion in your broccoli. God says it isn't wise to think that you have everything figured out or that nothing strange will ever happen. It will. But when it does, it's wonderful to remember that God is with you and can help you through it all.

When something unexpected happens, it's important to remember that it's sometimes caused by other people's choices. Sometimes, however, it's because *you've* made choices that don't honor God. And other times, the things you wanted to happen just can't happen yet.

During these strange moments, it can seem like you've found a scorpion in broccoli. You don't want it, hate seeing it, and wish you could hit a reset button to avoid the strangeness. Often, you can't. You've got to go through it. . .but God will go with you.

You may not have everything figured out, but God does. Trust Him instead.

I have lived through strange things, Lord. It can be frightening because it's not what I expected, and I don't know what will happen next. When I can't get comfortable, please help me remember everything is going to be alright—You know just what to do and just how to help me get past all the strange things I discover.

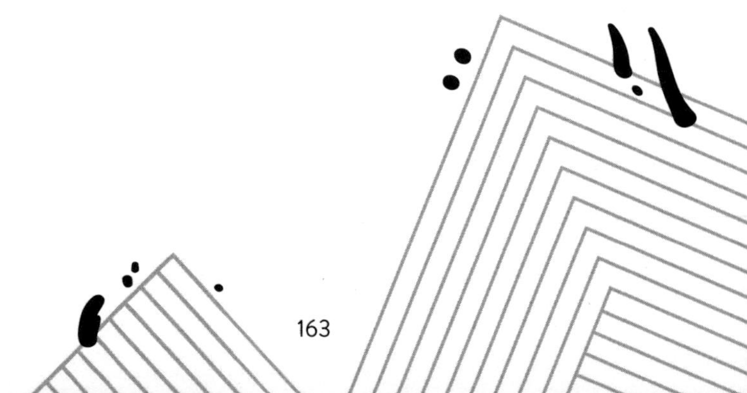

DAY 80

THE ARTIST

In the beginning God made from nothing
the heavens and the earth.

Genesis 1:1

Along the shores of Michigan, many winters bring an art show. When the wind blows, the temperature falls, and the snow swirls, God creates a world of unique and beautiful snow sculptures. It may be a complicated process, but it leaves beautiful art until warmer weather melts the cold sculptures.

In every season, you can find things that God made just because He wanted you to enjoy them. At the very beginning, He made the earth and sky. But He didn't stop. He thought you'd also like trees, animals, birds, and fish. He made mountains because boys like you might like to climb them. He made creeks, rivers, ponds, and oceans. He made the moon, stars, and planets. But He *still* didn't stop. God made flowers of all colors and shapes. Most of them smell really good. He also made insects, reptiles, and amphibians. And because God was certain you would enjoy it, He created a sunrise and sunset—and none of them are the same. He kept the surprises coming with canyons, geysers, and waterfalls.

God is an impressive artist. He not only created what you see but what you hear, smell, taste, and touch. He created language so people could understand each other but also so they could learn to understand Him. He also created music to make people think and allow them to respond to His goodness.

He paints the sky, plans earth's landscape, and fills the

oceans with beautiful and unusual creatures. There will never be another artist like God. The best any other artist can do is find inspiration from what God has already made. They can use paints made from His creation, and the people who enjoy the art are also made by God.

No matter what form of art you enjoy, it started with God's creativity.

Everywhere I look, I discover Your wonder, Father. You call this expression praise, and You say it's good. Your creation is good. Your art is amazing. And if this is earth, I can't wait to see heaven! Thank You for making all these things for me to enjoy. I want to enjoy it even more.

DAY 81

THE COLOR OF HOPE

Our hope comes from God. May He fill you with joy and peace because of your trust in Him. May your hope grow stronger by the power of the Holy Spirit.

ROMANS 15:13

If you've ever had to move, you know how sad losing your home can be. In your old house, you know where everything is and you have your favorite spots, so when it comes time to move, the final step can be really hard.

Huang lived in Taiwan and was told he would lose his home. He didn't want to move. The thought made him sad. But then he had an idea—an idea that many thought was very strange. In the time he had left in his home, he decided to give the place a new look. Huang painted the walls and doors with bright colors. Then he moved on to paint furniture, bookcases, and everything else inside and outside his home. When there was nothing left to paint on his house, he took more paint and started on his neighbors' homes (who'd also been told to leave).

College students who lived near Huang's house noticed the colorful neighborhood, and they began to show up to help paint. Finally, officials noticed, and they decided to save this neighborhood and turn it into a public park where people could look at the beautiful painting. Also, anyone who lived in the homes could stay!

Huang had hope. He believed that if he did something, then maybe he could keep his home. He had no idea if it would work, but he hoped.

God wants you to have hope in Him. But this hope is different—it's not just a wish. Instead, it is trusting God to do what He said He would do. Hope can make you sure that God loves you and will always take care of you. This hope makes it easier to get up each morning to face days that may not seem so great.

I want to be sure, God, that You'll be amazing. You tell me that it's true and that I can trust You, so help me believe that what You say is what You'll do. That's the kind of hope I need. . .and the kind of hope You give.

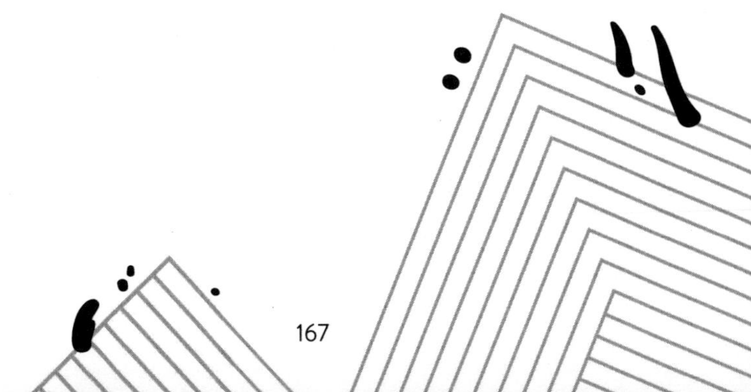

DAY 82

THE PROOF IS IN THE BELIEVING

"Good will come to the man who trusts in the Lord, and whose hope is in the Lord. He will be like a tree planted by the water, that sends out its roots by the river. It will not be afraid when the heat comes but its leaves will be green. It will not be troubled in a dry year, or stop giving fruit."

JEREMIAH 17:7–8

When Trey was four years old, he got a pet pig. He named the pig Snort. More than 20 years later, Snort was still living with Trey. He could have been the oldest pig in the world!

The problem was that Trey couldn't prove Snort was older than any other pig. Since he didn't have the right papers (like a birth certificate), nobody believed his claim. So was Snort actually the oldest pig? Because of a lack of evidence, the world will never know.

It can be hard to know something is true when people say, "Prove it!" People might ask you to prove God exists. But how do you do that? Will they be able to see Him? Can they ask Him questions and hear His response? God put today's verses in the Bible to help you understand that all the proof anyone needs is found in trusting Him first. In John 20:29, Jesus said, "Those are happy who have never seen Me and yet believe!"

People can believe God exists by just looking at what He does—that's all the proof they need. But this proof only comes after they believe it's true. Maybe God wants you to know that even if no one believes you, the fact that you believe Him is enough.

Trey has no birth certificate for Snort, but even if no one else ever believes him, he knows how special his pig was.

You can be satisfied knowing that God exists and that He's done great things for you.

It seems strange to think I have to believe before I see more of You, Lord. It's easier to do it the other way around. But You want me to know You're so trustworthy that there's never a good reason to doubt You.

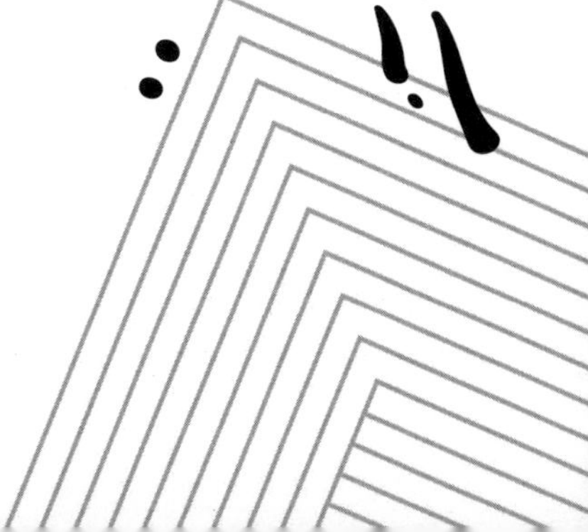

DAY 83

FOLLOWING SAUSAGE

The Lord has done great things for us and we are glad.
Psalm 126:3

Can you think of a good reason to fly a drone that's dangling cooked sausage? It could be a unique way to feed a pet, a fun challenge that makes you hungry, or a delivery to someone cooking on a grill. A rescue crew in England had a much different reason—and their reason was really good.

Millie was a smaller dog who loved exploring. One day, as she was walking by the ocean, she stumbled into some mud flats—areas that flood when high tide shows up. Rescuers couldn't reach the dog, but she could still walk on the mud flats because she didn't weigh very much. Then came the drone dangling the cooked sausage. The smell caught Millie's attention, and she followed the drone to safety.

God does some amazing things to help you. It may not be something you recognize right away—and you might even think it isn't a good thing. But it might just be something good that you don't understand yet. Think of Millie chasing a sausage. The dog had no idea she was in trouble or that she might die. So when rescuers got her attention, she was rescued—but all she was thinking about was a snack.

Be glad when God does great things. Take some time to think about how He's helped you. Sometimes, you won't notice His help until the danger is over. That will be a perfect time to thank God if you haven't already. He will do for you what you can't do for yourself.

If people can rescue a dog with fried sausage and a drone, imagine all the creative ways God can help you! Follow God because He leads, walk His direction because He knows where He's going, and ask questions because He has answers.

Let Him rescue because you need to be rescued. Sometimes, it's just as easy as following sausage!

I know I haven't paid enough attention when You help me, Father. Give me the wisdom to see what You do for me and then to thank You for everything. I love You and want to follow You every day of my life.

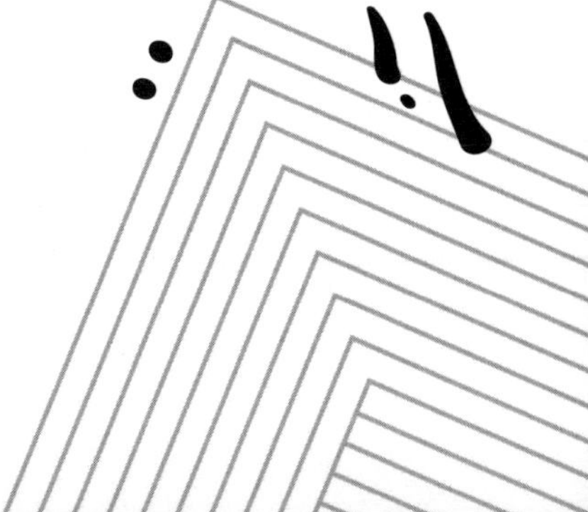

DAY 84

BEAUTY BEHIND THE WALLS

For You made the parts inside me. You put me together inside my mother. I will give thanks to You, for the greatness of the way I was made brings fear. Your works are great and my soul knows it very well.

Psalm 139:13–14

Nick and Lisa had no idea that the old building they bought hid a secret that would bring joy and wonder to their small town in Washington. The couple bought the building to create a new business. As they were remodeling the house, Nick became curious about a very long wall. He checked behind the old plaster, and what he saw changed everything: a painting that was 60 feet long and 20 feet high!

The building had once been a movie theater, and the painting had been part of its theater days. They soon found a second painting on the opposite wall. Now, these restored paintings are a celebrated part of their business.

God made you a masterpiece, and He hid treasure inside you for you to discover. You might have to break down walls of mistrust and anger to find it, and it will take forgiveness and compassion to restore. But God gave it to you, and He doesn't want it to stay hidden from view—He wants others to see it.

Let God remove the walls that have been hiding the masterpiece that you are. Hiding doesn't help anyone know God better. Staying out of view may seem safe, but it never allows people to praise God for what He does—or experience His goodness for themselves.

God has done incredible things in you. Why would you ever want to keep His goodness from showing through? Put God on display—not your good works or ideas. You can't be good enough on your own.

You are a masterpiece because that's the way God made you.

When I hide who You made me to be, I might be hiding from You, God. Maybe I'm not sure You can do something amazing in my life. Help me trust that You have made me a masterpiece and that You want me to learn what You've done. I don't want to hide You anymore.

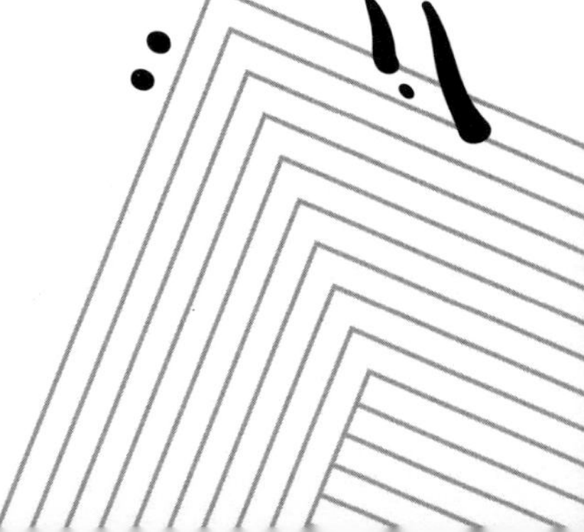

DAY 85

LET THE FOX NAP ELSEWHERE

I am not saying I need anything. I have learned to be happy with whatever I have. I know how to get along with little and how to live when I have much. I have learned the secret of being happy at all times. If I am full of food and have all I need, I am happy. If I am hungry and need more, I am happy.

PHILIPPIANS 4:11–12

Some things are just hard to believe, even when you see them. That's probably what some teachers in London thought when they saw a fox napping on a couch in the teachers' lounge at school. Earlier that day, some workers had opened the outside doors—and that's when the fox had wandered in.

The teachers who discovered the sleeping fox quietly closed the door and locked it until animal rescue crews could help the fox find a better place to sleep.

It's possible this fox had become *complacent*. That means he was satisfied but sloppy in the decisions he made. The couch seemed like a great place to take a nap, so he didn't care how strange it looked. He should have learned to be *content*. This would've meant being satisfied with what he already had—outside.

You can choose to be satisfied with things you know aren't good for you. But when that happens, you won't be content. Being content means you'll listen to God. Being complacent means you listen only to what you want to do.

God is pleased to see you grateful for what you have. Being

content means whatever happens to you doesn't change how you see God's goodness. It can make you happy to trust God and obey His rules. Being complacent, however, leaves you shrugging your shoulders and saying "Whatever" when you actually need to do something.

You have a choice—choose contentment!

I don't want to treat my time with You as if it doesn't matter, Lord. I don't want to be like a fox who takes a nap in a place that isn't safe. Help me be content but never complacent. May my life look like Your heart. May my feet follow in Your steps. I want that kind of satisfaction.

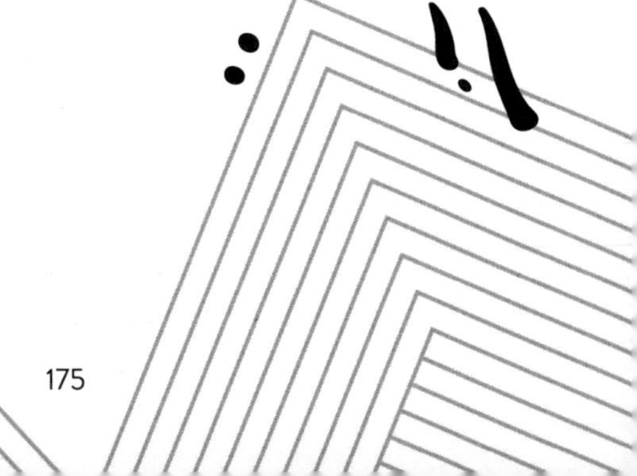

DAY 86

THE BALLOON BOUNCE

Two are better than one, because they have good pay for their work. For if one of them falls, the other can help him up. But it is hard for the one who falls when there is no one to lift him up.

Ecclesiastes 4:9–10

There's a game that you've probably played for most of your life, even if you don't know what it's called. This game is played when people try to keep a balloon from hitting the ground. Each player bounces the balloon upward, and both players try to keep it in the air. It's a really fun way to pass time.

People in Spain have come up with what they call the Balloon World Cup. (They *still* haven't named the game yet!) Here, "professionals" from all over the world show up to bop a balloon in search of inflated glory. Apparently, teams from dozens of countries have all known what it's like to get bored at family get-togethers, so they show up to play. . .and they play to win.

Playing mindless games with friends is so much better than playing any other game by yourself. It feels pretty good to be that comfortable around a friend.

God made these kinds of friendships for a reason. After all, being alone feels horrible. You need encouragement, but when you're alone, you don't always get it. You need a helping hand, but no one's close. You need to hear that everything will get better, but there's no one around.

Friendships are important because they can remind you

that God has always been with you—and that you can talk to Him as easily as you can talk to your closest friend. Friendships can even remind you to be a good friend to others. When friends get together to work on a job, things move along at a speedier, more enjoyable pace.

Why be alone when you can make friends?

When You bring a good friend for me to meet,
I remember that You're good, Father. Friendships are
important to You, and they're important to me too.
They are gifts that I don't want to live without.

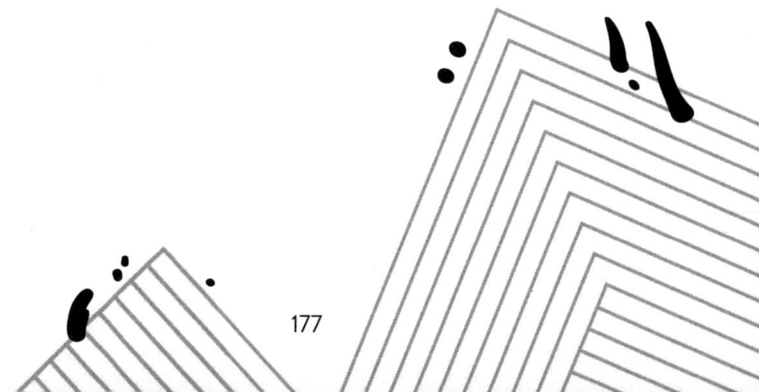

DAY 87

THE RIGHT RESPONSE

Be happy with those who are happy.
Be sad with those who are sad.
Romans 12:15

In Mississippi, 77 tough and ready contestants step up to catch fish in the annual Fishing Rodeo, which was designed for special needs children. Young kids have waited weeks to take this field trip, and their parents, brothers, and sisters are enjoying it too. But not everyone will catch a fish. As a result, tears will be shed. That's when family and friends step in and follow Romans 12:15.

It's confusing when people are sad, but you insist on being happy. They might wonder if you really understand their sadness. On the other hand, if you're sad when they give you good news, they might think you don't care.

Even if you're sad about something that has happened to you, you can be happy for others. And being happy for yourself is great, but you can also be kind and show sympathy for your friends. The last thing God wants you to do is to make friends think their feelings don't matter to you.

Think about what it would be like if God treated you that way. Would it make sense for God to tell jokes when you pray for help when you're struggling? Would it be kind for God to say your good news is no big deal?

If you don't expect God to act like that, then why would you act like that toward a friend? Those friends will remember how you acted when they shared the news. A bad response can make some friends stop being friends.

Be the friend that other people need. Take the time to listen, and try to see life through their eyes. It could be very good—or very bad—and they might just need to know someone cares enough to agree with how they feel.

Thank You for standing with me, God. My bad days don't chase You away, and my good days give me a reason to be grateful. I'm better because You're becoming more important to me. You listen to the good, the bad, and the not very great moments I face.

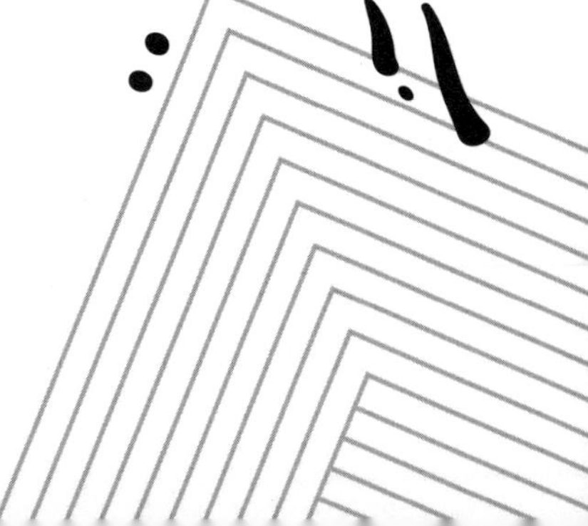

DAY 88

THE GOOD YOU CAN DO

Let us give thanks all the time to God through Jesus Christ. Our gift to Him is to give thanks. Our lips should always give thanks to His name. Remember to do good and help each other. Gifts like this please God.

Hebrews 13:15–16

Steve is a stock car racer who wants to help people. He loves being a dad, and he's inspired by his sons. Cameron, his oldest boy, was diagnosed with severe aplastic anemia—a disease that affects the bones. He needed a bone marrow transplant, and it had to be a perfect match. That's where his younger brother, Harrison, came in. He was a perfect match, and Harrison wanted to help his big brother.

Steve took time away from the racetrack to be a dad and support his son's recovery. It just seemed the only good choice he could make. Now, Steve and his wife spend time raising awareness of blood disorders like the one Cameron faced, and they encourage people to consider becoming part of the National Bone Marrow Registry.

Helping someone you love might come naturally. Helping someone you don't know, however, might be a bit harder. But what about doing good for someone you don't like? That can be tough!

But that's what God asks us to do. He's pleased when you see someone in need and then help out. He cares about the way you treat other people.

God will never ask you to do something He won't do. If

He won't do something, then He probably doesn't want you doing it. If He asks you to do something (like helping others), it's because it's something He already does. His example is wise, honorable, and helpful.

Trust God's plan for how you should do good things. He will give you the opportunity to help others. You get to choose whether you'll take the opportunity. . .or just watch someone else do what you could have done.

Harrison helped Cameron—who will you help?

I sometimes miss the opportunities You send, Lord. Help me to never turn down the chance to follow You in doing good and helping other people. You've helped me, so help me do good things for other people.

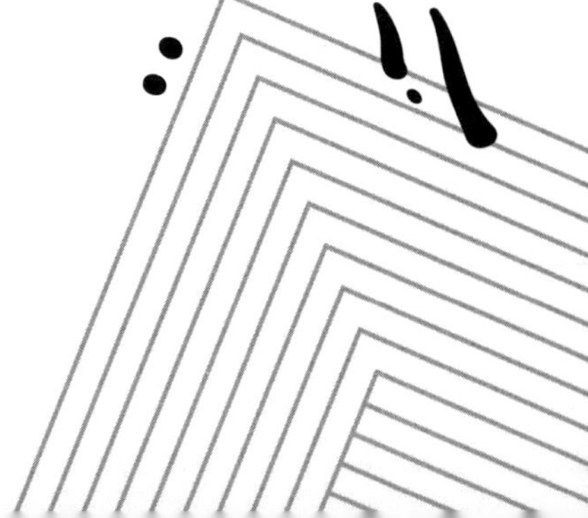

DAY 89

GOOD JOBS CAN BE BETTER

Christian brothers, keep your minds thinking about whatever is true, whatever is respected, whatever is right, whatever is pure, whatever can be loved, and whatever is well thought of. If there is anything good and worth giving thanks for, think about these things. Keep on doing all the things you learned and received and heard from me. Do the things you saw me do. Then the God Who gives peace will be with you.

PHILIPPIANS 4:8–9

A food delivery service in Texas was looking for a taco fan to fill a unique job—they wanted someone to discover the best tacos in Texas. The reward? A whopping *10,000* dollars! This company made sure their new employee had a place to stay, a bunch of food, and a means of transportation as the worker traveled all over Texas.

Not all jobs are the same. Some people love their jobs, and some people don't. You might ask God to help you decide what job to do when you are old enough to work, or you might just pick one and give it a try. No matter what choice you make, God will give you another choice after you make that one. Even if you don't keep this job, you can think about the good things God mentions in Philippians 4:8. When you do, it'll change the way you think about your job.

Even when you do something for your family, try to find the truth, respect, right choices, purity, love, good, and grateful things in your job. See how much you can find, and discover why it's a great thing to be positive while you work.

You might not get to taste tacos in Texas (as good as that might sound!), but you *can* follow God's instruction and respond in a way that will gain His approval. Doing this can help you look for the bright side, even when it's easier to notice things that are false, disliked, wrong, sinful, hated, and rude.

See? God's instructions for thinking are much better.

I need to control the way I think and the things I think about, Father. Give me control over my thoughts and help me bring Your way of thinking into everything that I do.

DAY 90

GOD'S KIND OF BRAVERY

"I am the Vine and you are the branches. Get your life from Me. Then I will live in you and you will give much fruit. You can do nothing without Me."

John 15:5

Evie faced a threat. . .and helped rescue a friend in the process. This six-year-old girl was at her neighbor's house playing with a three-year-old boy she met that day. Her babysitter, Sarah, came to get Evie because it looked like a storm was coming.

That's when the dog attacked.

Evie didn't run, cry, or scream; she just stepped between the angry dog and her new three-year-old friend. Amazingly, this worked! The dog, realizing he wasn't welcome, left. Evie's elementary school later celebrated her bravery and kindness, and most people who know Evie weren't surprised by her good deed.

This girl was incredibly brave. She's not the first, and she won't be the last.

You too can be brave. This might not mean standing up to a raging dog—no, all it means is doing something you didn't think you could do. It might be as simple as standing up for someone who's bullied. You don't need to fight anyone, just remind the bullies that what they're doing isn't right. You might be brave enough to tell an adult about a student who's being picked on. You might even tell someone about Jesus. Sometimes, you have to be very brave to do that.

This kind of bravery is the life God gives you. When you

live for Him, He makes sure you'll have everything you need to do what He asks. He's always with you, and every good thing you'll ever do is just a repeat of what He's already done. When you're kind and loving, it'll be easier to see God as kind and loving, especially when you let people know He's the reason you act the way you do.

Your good choice might just give someone else a reason to believe that a good God exists.

May I stand up for people who can't, God. May my choices give people a reason to look for You. May my heart follow You into great choices. Keep helping me be brave.

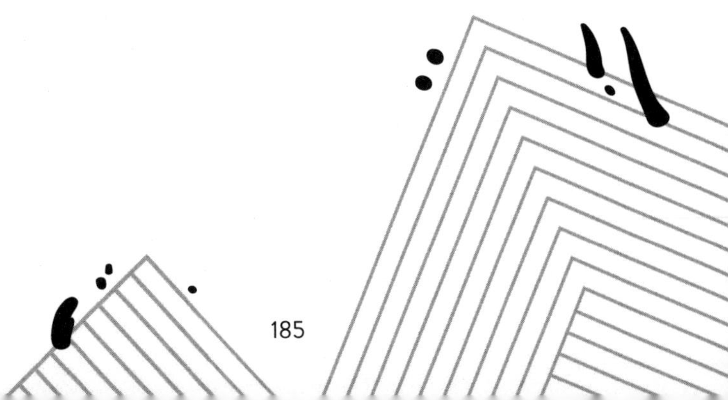

DAY 91

THE WEEDS TUMBLE

Have nothing to do with your old sinful life. It was sinful because of being fooled into following bad desires. Let your minds and hearts be made new. You must become a new person and be God-like. Then you will be made right with God and have a true holy life.

Ephesians 4:22–24

Steve lives in Wyoming. Sometimes, he searches for two perfect tumbleweeds and stacks them to make a Christmas tree. People always want to see what he creates. And in neighboring Utah, other people are finding new ways to deal with this pesky, rolling weed.

In spring, these weeds start rolling through neighborhoods and clogging roads. Several tons of tumbleweeds have to be burned or put in landfills. That's always hard work.

People are finding unique ways to decorate these "useless" weeds and put them up for sale online. It seems some people, especially those who live in cities where no tumbleweed can be found, really like this idea! Decorating their home with these creations causes people to notice and ask questions.

Most people don't think tumbleweeds are beautiful, especially if you have hundreds of them piled against your fence. For others, these western weeds seem more creative and decorative. As the old saying goes, "One man's trash is another man's treasure."

Taking something old and making it new is just what God does. He's the best at it. People renovate homes, and God replaces hard hearts. People make new things from old furniture, and God makes new things from old lives. He makes an ordinary thing into something it could never be without His help. And God helps you too! You are (and always will be) God's treasure. God has never seen you as disposable trash. Nothing stops Him from loving you.

You must become new. It's God's best plan for you, and it's always where you start. New is important. After all, God won't settle for what's old in you. You need God's new—so say goodbye to the old.

It's sometimes hard to let go of the old, Lord. I feel like I might lose myself if I let You change me. But You promise something so much better. So take me and make me new.

DAY 92

DO YOU WANT TO?

Christian brothers, I ask you from my heart to give your bodies to God because of His loving-kindness to us. Let your bodies be a living and holy gift given to God. He is pleased with this kind of gift. This is the true worship that you should give Him.

Romans 12:1

It's doubtful that a police officer has ever woke up one morning and thought, *I wonder if I'll have to arrest a goat today?* But sometimes, duty calls in unexpected ways.

The Tallahassee Police Department once responded to a call that involved a goat who was causing problems in an apartment complex. This wily goat wasn't content to roam outdoors. No, he was arrested after running down a hallway!

Who knew a police officer's work could involve goats?

You've read about how adventurous the Christian life can be. You may find yourself in circumstances you never expected—like a police officer chasing a goat. But these unexpected events are usually the most memorable. Some people go on missions trips to countries they've never visited before. They help people they've never met and build things they've never built.

God will take you places, but it won't be because you know what you're doing—it'll be because you're willing. Your willingness is more important than your skills. Why? If God asks you to do something, it's because His help is always better than your effort. He can do what you can't.

Because God is kind, you should use your willingness as a gift He can use. And He will! You don't have to be an expert at anything to be useful to God. He pays more attention to your heart than anything else. While He can (and will) use your skills, He's more interested in whether you want to do what He asks.

Do you want to?

It's easy to turn people down when I don't know how to do what they ask, Father. When You ask me the same thing, I need to remember that You can also teach me what I need to do. You can do what I can't, so encourage me to be willing to adventure with You.

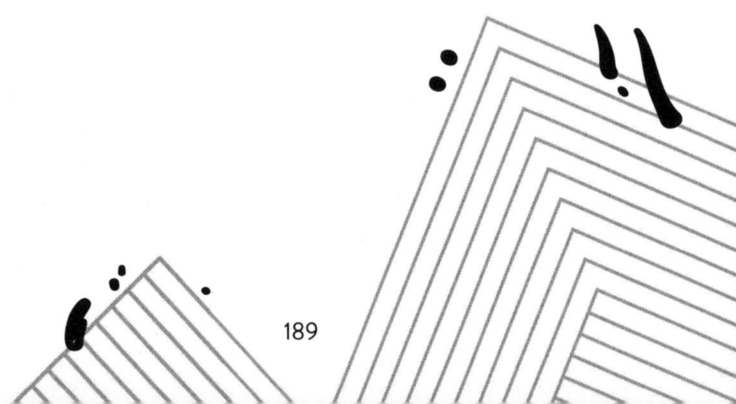

DAY 93

REACTIONS TO THE SIN ALLERGY

[Jesus] said, "Whatever comes out of a man is what makes the man sinful. From the inside, out of the heart of men come bad thoughts. . .killing other people, stealing, wanting something that belongs to someone else, doing wrong, lying. . .having a mind that is always looking for sin, speaking against God, thinking you are better than you are and doing foolish things."

MARK 7:20–22

There are all kinds of things you can be allergic to. Some of the usual "bad guys" include pollen, animal dander, dust mites, and all kinds of food (milk, shellfish, nuts, and so on). You can also be allergic to certain medicines, household chemicals, and mold.

There are many other allergies that don't affect most people. Did you know some people are allergic to water? Others are allergic to the sun, weather, electricity, and coins. There are even people who are allergic to the smell of fish! Each of these allergies has symptoms, and anyone who experiences them is not a fan.

Breaking God's law is a bit like having an allergy. When you sin, you have to live with the symptoms. Often, other people see those symptoms too. They might notice you're angry and disrespectful. They might see that you're rude and unloving. They may realize that you don't want to talk about things you once loved and that you've become less friendly.

When these symptoms show up, it's time to recognize your sin allergy and seek treatment. Thankfully, you have a good God with a great prescription. Mark 7:20–22 lists some common situations that lead to the sin allergy, and the way to get rid of these symptoms is to stop hanging out with sin. Start looking for God instead. He has so many things for you to do—and you'll never be allergic to any of them.

Why stay in a place that keeps you miserable? Come back to God and keep coming back every time you have a sin allergy. Only He can help you feel better.

---

*I don't like how I feel when I break Your rules, God—
and nobody else likes how I act, either. I don't want to
live with these symptoms. I need to accept Your help
and feel better. Free me from my allergic reaction.*

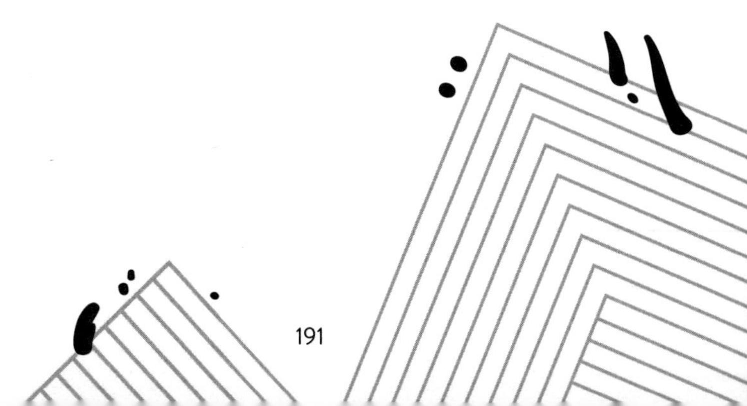

DAY 94

FINISHING WELL

I have fought a good fight. I have finished the work I was to do. I have kept the faith. There is a crown which comes from being right with God. The Lord, the One Who will judge, will give it to me on that great day when He comes again.

2 TIMOTHY 4:7–8

Some people start life making bad choices, but they finish well. Some start bad and finish bad. Some people start pretty good and then get worse from there. But some start pretty good, and with God's help, they keep making good choices.

Abby had a very good idea. She started an organization for young people that stressed the importance of helping each other. Everyone thought Abby's idea was a good one.

But then Abby got cancer.

Years later, Emmy and Alex—Abby's younger siblings—stepped up to restart the organization after Abby's death. This program highlights good deeds done in a community. No matter how old the idea was, it was still a good one.

When God starts something, He keeps working until it's done. If He starts by using you, but then you stop helping, it doesn't stop God from finishing what He started. He may just choose someone else.

You have lots of chances to be helpful, but it's really easy to leave when the going gets rough. Sometimes, the Christian life has challenges you may not want to face—even though you have help from God. You might be very willing to let someone else take the wheel. On the other hand, you might be so prideful that you won't accept help even if someone offers. In that case, maybe God knows you need help. Maybe God has something new for you to do. Maybe God knows you could use a friend.

If you started the race well, it's great to finish well. If you started badly, you can still get up and run! Wherever you are, you need to remember to keep moving toward God's finish line, accepting whatever help God gives.

God will always finish well. Will you?

I might try but fail, Lord. I might try to do things all alone. Or I might refuse to start. Help me make the right choices so that I keep getting closer to You.

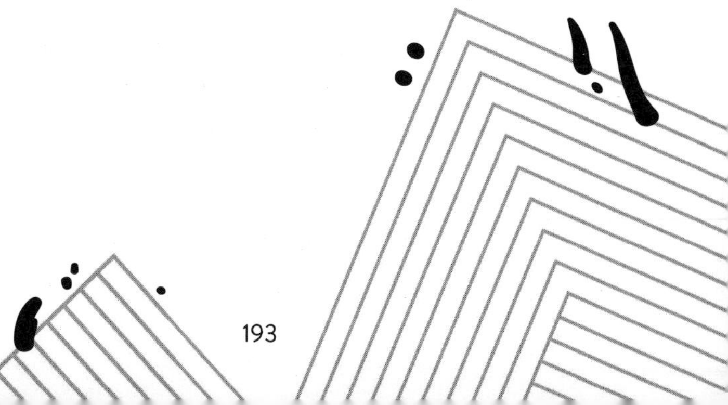

DAY 95

TIRED. SAD. DEPRESSED.

How can they call on [Jesus] if they have not put their trust in Him? And how can they put their trust in Him if they have not heard of Him? And how can they hear of Him unless someone tells them? And how can someone tell them if he is not sent? The Holy Writings say, "The feet of those who bring the Good News are beautiful."

ROMANS 10:14–15

It's easy to find bad news. It may not be everywhere, but it sure sounds like it. News channels pick all the bad things and share each bit of badness. It can make you feel sad, nervous, and totally stressed out. Bad news can also make it easy to forget a good God. It's hard to sleep well if you're always wondering when the next round of bad news will come. It can make you worry—a lot.

Experts say that boys like you need good news. It makes hard days easier to live through and lets you know you don't have to chase bad news all the time.

You might know that the first four books of the New Testament are called *Gospels*. They are stories about Jesus' life—what He did and what He said. The word *gospel* means "good news." So if you want to read some really good news, consider reading Matthew, Mark, Luke, or John. They include the good news story of how Jesus came, grew, died, and rose from the dead. This act of love was God's gift to you—and *that* is good news. These "good news books" won't make you tired, sad, or depressed. In fact, they might make you more interested in sharing this news with whomever needs it!

Take this good news with you. Walk like you're carrying an important message—you are! Set bad news aside because you have better news to share. Bad news makes you tired, sad, and depressed, but God's good news makes you energized, joyful, and filled to the top with hope.

I love good news, Father. You have some, so I want to hear it, know it, and share it. This is my prayer. This is my hope. You are my God.

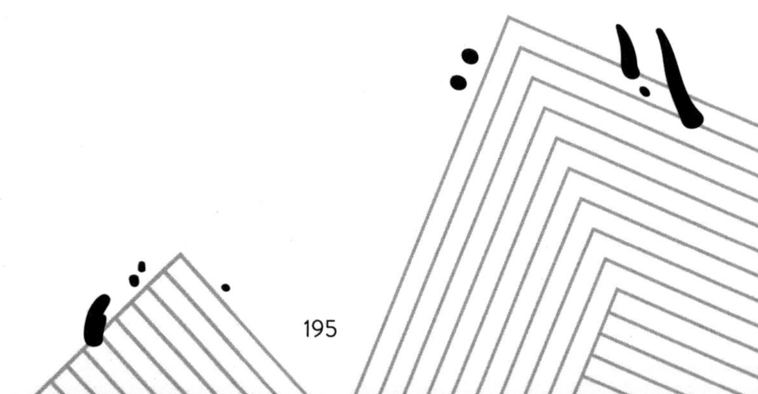

DAY 96

THE SURFING HOUSE

I do one thing. I forget everything that is behind me and look forward to that which is ahead of me. My eyes are on the crown. I want to win the race and get the crown of God's call from heaven through Christ Jesus.

PHILIPPIANS 3:13–14

What if someone gave you a house for free? That would be quite a gift. What if someone told you that in order to get the house, you'd have to move it? Well, that's a lot harder. But that's what happened to Kirk and Danielle. Their dream home was theirs to take—it was just in the wrong place.

They decided to fix the problem by removing the house from its shoreline view. How? By putting barrels under the two-story house and floating it on the lake more than half a mile to its new home!

The couple floated the house, dried things out, and remodeled things. They're just thrilled that their home isn't a pile of sticks on the other side of the bay.

Life can seem like trusting a house to a bunch of barrels, hoping it doesn't end up at the bottom of the lake. There isn't much about life that seems easy, but God says that following Jesus is the best way to bring you across the waves to your new home. Kirk and Danielle did that with a wooden home, but God has something so much better waiting for you.

God's good ideas are more important than the ideas you have. He knows how things will turn out if you follow Him. But if you follow what you want to do without asking what God wants, you'll always be unsure.

The more you spend time with God learning what He wants, the more you'll begin to want the same things. Suddenly, what you want will begin to look like what God wants.

What happens next is something *way* better than a surfing house.

You say I should forget what happened in the past, God. I can't change it, and You've forgiven it. Help me look ahead to the good things You have waiting for me. I can't wait to be amazed.

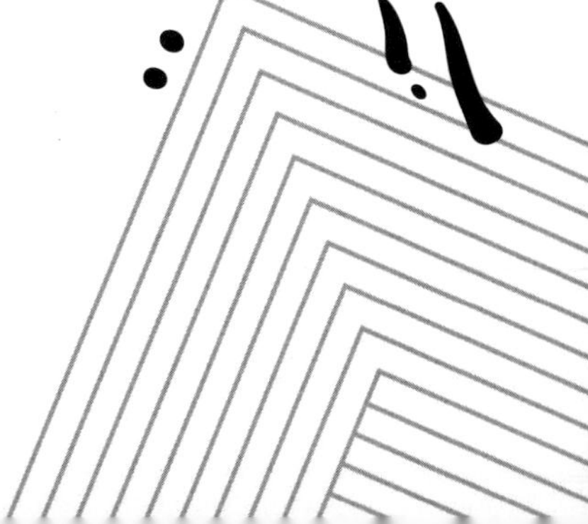

DAY 97

ACCEPTING THE PROMISE

"I followed the Lord my God with all my heart. So Moses promised on that day, 'For sure the land where your foot has stepped will be a gift to you and your children forever. Because you have followed the Lord my God with all your heart.' Now see, the Lord has let me live, as He said, these forty-five years since the Lord spoke this word to Moses while Israel walked in the desert. Today I am eighty-five years old. I am as strong today as I was the day Moses sent me. I am as strong now as I was then."

Joshua 14:8–11

Debbie is a star athlete in college. She plays golf and hits mid-eighties in every tournament she plays. She's a consistent player, an encourager, a sophomore. . .and 63 years old. She's 40 years older than anyone else on the team, including the coach!

Debbie always wanted to go to college, but life brought a family, and she became very busy. After her husband died, she started college—something she was certain she'd never be able to do.

In the Bible, Caleb had big plans too. God promised a place for His people to live, but they were too scared. As a result, they couldn't have the land for more than 40 years. Caleb, however, was one of two men who thought they should move into the land. After all, God had given it to them as a gift. So in Joshua 14:8–11, Caleb—who was now an old man—was set free to discover the home he'd dreamt of for so long.

He said it was God who made him strong enough to do what younger men were frightened to do. Caleb believed God had a home for him in a place he once visited, so he didn't care how scared everyone else was.

Spend time learning about God's promises, and don't stop believing that He'll keep them. Even when you're as old as Caleb, God will still be keeping promises. He'll never stop.

Thanks for never breaking a promise, Lord. Thanks for surprising people, no matter how old they are, with good things. Thanks for showing Your love in very personal ways. Thanks for promising a forever home.

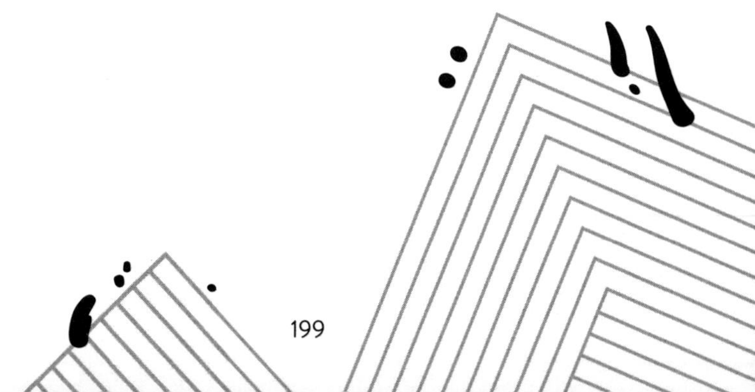

DAY 98

AN IMPRESSIVE TRADE

God bought you with a great price. So honor God with your body. You belong to Him.
1 CORINTHIANS 6:20

When hard times strike, people often come up with new ideas. Some of these ideas work, and some do not. This is called *innovation*. If you think innovation sounds a little bit like invention, you're on the right track. Both words involve creating something entirely new.

Janur owns a restaurant in Indonesia. But when hard times came to his country, people could not afford to eat out as much. Business was slow, and other restaurants were closing. But as Janur looked at the streets in his town, he noticed that trash seemed to be everywhere.

Suddenly, he had an idea.

The restaurant owner wondered if people would come to his restaurant if they could get food for something they no longer needed—trash. Sounds like a rotten trade, right? But Janur didn't want just any trash. He would trade food for plastic.

His idea spread to 200 villages, and people traded 500 tons of plastic for food. He's been able to keep his restaurant open, and people have been enjoying his good food while they get rid of some trash.

You might think that this trade is unfair, but just think of all the people it has helped! God makes a similar trade with you every day. He trades your sin for His perfection. You get riches that you'd never deserve by giving God your rotten life choices. . .just like trash in the street. But God is willing to make that trade. You might want to try to pay Him back somehow, but the only way you can really do that is to say thank you. Then you can follow and obey a perfect God.

Oh, it's also a very good thing if you tell others how they can make the same trade. They need this impressive trade as much as you do!

I have always received more from You than I can ever give back, Father. Thank You for doing something for me that I can't do on my own. May I love You enough to make this good news known to anyone who's looking for something that only You can give.

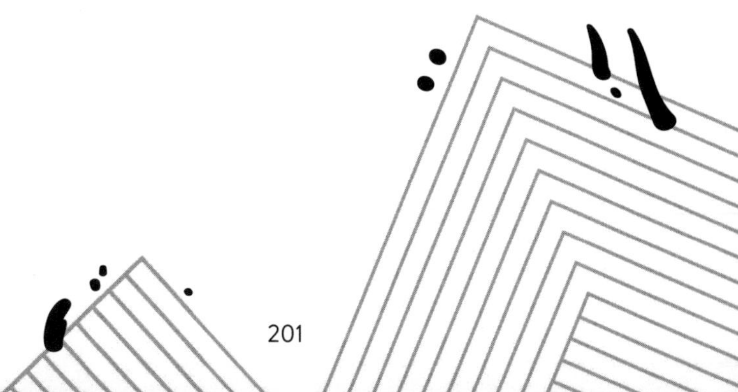

DAY 99

BETTER PEST CONTROL

The Lord is my light and the One Who saves me. Whom should I fear? The Lord is the strength of my life. Of whom should I be afraid? . . . For in the day of trouble He will keep me safe in His holy tent. In the secret place of His tent He will hide me. He will set me high upon a rock.

Psalm 27:1, 5

When people grow grapes, they can have problems with mice, rats, and gophers. These rodents love eating the fruit. . .and they can damage more than just the grapes. Farmers have used plenty of chemicals to control the rodents, but that can get expensive. Thankfully, a more ancient method is more useful: pest control owls.

Farmers in California put up nesting boxes for owls, and the owls enjoy the free house. The owls then protect the area around their houses by leaving at night (which is what owls do) and using the vineyard as a grocery store. The owls don't eat grapes, but they eat the small things that do eat grapes.

Life is full of pests. They hang out and make life hard. These pests can include the choices you make, the angry words you hear and speak, and the things that stop you from following God. You can try harder, promise to do better, or even ask a friend to help. But none of these methods will be as effective as allowing God to step in and provide pest control.

God knows that His enemy, Satan, is also a pest who can make a mess of things, so God works to limit this pest. Psalm 27 says that God is your light, strength, and salvation. He's not a pest—He's your protector. He's not a nuisance—He wants to see you grow strong. God is not your enemy.

Today, spend some time thanking Him for His willingness to help and provide personal pest control.

Thank You for being my friend, God. Thanks for keeping pests away as I walk with You. There will always be pests, but with You, there are fewer of them. Only You can help stop them before they do so much damage.

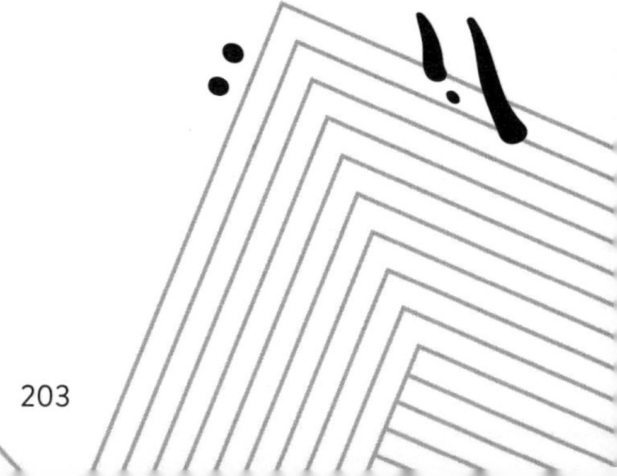

DAY 100

THE AROMA OF ADVENTURE

The Good News is like a sweet smell to those who hear it. We are a sweet smell of Christ that reaches up to God. It reaches out to those who are being saved from the punishment of sin and to those who are still lost in sin. It is the smell of death to those who are lost in sin. It is the smell of life to those who are being saved from the punishment of sin.

2 Corinthians 2:14–16

What kind of sniffer do bugs have? Certain smells seem to attract bugs, so there's plenty of evidence that they use their little noses well.

One day, scientists decided to use scent as a way to keep bugs off plants—so they created a scent that smells like fear. Insects recognize this scent as a predator. It immediately convinces them there are better plants to munch elsewhere.

To humans, the smell is sweet. But to bugs? Apparently, they think it's cruel and unusual punishment.

Don't end this 100-day journey without remembering that your life either attracts people to God or makes them run away. Your life either pleases God or causes Him to send you back to class to relearn important lessons.

If you were serious when you opened this book, then you may be further along your faith journey than you were on day one. But don't stop now! Keep exploring God's instructions long after you close this book.

Don't look at the time in this book as some kind of class

you take and then forget. God is a life-altering choice, and 100 days is a very small step in a forever journey. There's more to come, and you might even decide to come back to this book and read it again sometime. The stories and Bible verses speak truth, help you remember, and encourage you to keep moving forward, even when it's easier to quit.

Make your life a sweet-smelling adventure for God!

I want my life to make people want to know You, Lord. I want my choices to look like Yours. I want my life to say I'm learning more, sharing more, and becoming more like You.

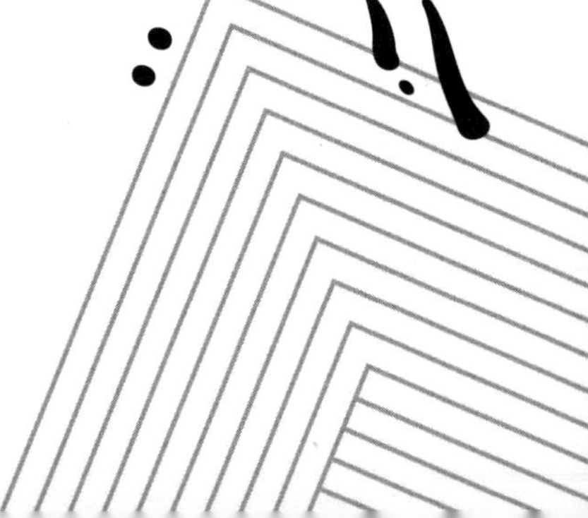

SCRIPTURE INDEX

Old Testament

New Testament